THE TOOLS AND MODULES OF

DIGITAL

MARKETING

A DEFINATIVE GUIDE TO LEARNING THE ART OF DIGITAL MARKETING FOR BEGINNERS

VISHAW DEEPAK

Disclaimer

Dedicated to you

CONTENTS

PREFACE

I feel great pleasure in presenting this book on "Digital Marketing" for those who want to learn the art of digital marketing. This book is written in a pretty simplistic style. I believe this will be beneficial to you.

This book has been designed to integrate with the skilled credentials in digital promoting to provide comprehensive learning expertise. Every chapter relates to a module within the course and also the book provides complete coverage of the digital marketing course.

To make it more beneficial at every level, massive numbers of different important tools and several modules with a detailed description has been added. Although every effort has been made to eliminate omissions and errors, yet if the readers find certain omissions or errors, their every constructive suggestion will be welcomed.

I want to create learning simple, accessible, and convenient. That's why I developed this textbook. It's an all-inclusive introductory guide that may teach you everything you would like to understand to start your digital marketing career. you'll read it chronologically or prioritize the chapters that interest you most; like our courses, this book was created to permit you to check during your own time and at your own pace, and you'll always refer thereto whenever you would like to!

I am very thankful for my publishers for their sincere efforts in bringing out the first edition of this book. I am also thankful to the editorial and publishing professionals for their keen interest and support in bringing out this edition of the present form.

Nevertheless a special thanks to my family and to my dearest friend Pratima Singh who continuously inspire me to greatness, her faith cause me to lift myself to a new level.

I have the sound wish and best of luck to this book and publisher as well.

-Author

x

INTRODUCTION OF DIGITAL MARKETING

The way people interact has transformed in recent years since online media has become an integral part of our daily lives. These additional features caused a change in business strategies and customer relations. Learn the solution to these problems - Digital Marketing!

DIGITAL MARKETING

The advent and development of the Internet have forced businesses to grow, digitalize, and adapt to new conditions. This phenomenon affected marketing and advertising in the same way, as standard advertising channels, strategies, and techniques did no longer promote a certain business brand.

This is a specific set of techniques that uses digital (digital) channels for advertising or - the Internet. The widest possible online audience can reach by using various advertising methods and channels.

At the beginning of the millennium, WEB 2.0 appeared, and with it concepts such as search engines, bots, artificial intelligence, process automation, virtual reality, and many others. The Internet continues to move in a clear direction - collaboration with consumers. The building blocks of digital marketing are also undergoing metamorphoses that continue today.

Social media is emerging, and the people there are a contingent of potential customers. The business quickly orientated itself in this situation and adopted the fresh ways of advertising - paid and organic. When a digital marketer hears the phrase "Advertising campaign" he immediately thinks of several things - product, target audience, budget/cost, result, and optimization.

OPTIMIZATION AND DESIGN

Attracting targeted traffic to a particular website, whether it's an online store, an information site, or a personal blog must be accompanied by well-optimized content and intriguing design. This applies to landing pages and to all other products and information pages. However, who would want to get into the following situation:

You are running a successful advertising campaign, the traffic to your site is increasing, but it is slow and difficult to navigate, users do not stay on our page. As a result, the advertising campaign becomes ineffective, our costs are not justified and we miss the opportunity for new sales.

TARGETING AND RETARGETING

With the development of technology, various tools appear to collect comprehensive information for consumers, which helps us to segment them more appropriately according to their tastes and interests.

Through the so-called "Cookies" we can understand more about the behavior of our visitors. This online information comprises data about sites viewed, searches performed, subsequent ads, and more.

When retargeting, we use the information already collected about consumer tastes and needs. A CELTA is to remind our potential customers about our services.

When you target and advertise your goal is one - to satisfy the need and need of a certain contingent of people from a certain product or service. Therefore, let the style of the message be individual, the message be personal. This way, your offer has a better chance of being considered and bringing in new customers.

THINK BIG!

Nowadays it is almost unthinkable not to be online! How else would a person from another city find out that you have a business, that you have a certain product or offer certain services? Ad "word of mouth" is useful, but often not enough. So think big, plan your online marketing strategy and create a long-term action plan. Start by building a corporate website, optimizing it, collecting an email list for campaigns, taking part in social networks. So it will not delay the positive results!

MODULE 1
SEARCH ENGINE OPTIMIZATION

WHAT IS SEARCH ENGINE OPTIMIZATION?

Search engine optimization (Search Engine Optimization) or SEO is a strategic plan to put your website at the top of the search engine ranking. This will increase the number of people who see your website and increase the number of viewers on your website. SEO is not a fixed technique because each type of business is different. But there are some good practices that you should know and follow.

Effective SEO applications can help you beat competitors. A Net Market Share survey (in August 2016) found that Google is the market leader in search engine data providers. With 71.11% of all searches on the Google platform, The pie chart above shows the other half of the data search engine, which is the market share of Bing, Baidu, Yahoo, and other service providers.

Overall, internet users around the world search for information using Google about 3.5 million times a day and 1.2 billion times a year. SEO helps countless people who may become your customers. Your business is considered a great opportunity that you should not miss.

THE BENEFITS OF SEO

Search engine optimization is a very complex but effective way to stay in the market competition. Because search engines like Google, Bing, Yahoo, are the primary choices of people, to search for something online these days. And here, search engine optimization plays an important role in online marketing.

SEO helps you create a better and user friendly website

For starters, SEO can help you create a better, faster, and easier website when viewed from a user perspective. Search engine optimization is, in fact, closer to working with users than search engines.

When your users are happy, search engines are happy too. This happiness is related to presenting the information they are looking for to the users in the most qualitative way.

Ensures you find new customers and grow

One of the main goals of a we bsite can be explained by increasing and differentiating the customer base. It is a fact that businesses that own a website grow twice as fast as those that do not.

SEO helps you get better rankings on your search engine results pages, which results in more targeted visits and more customer engagement.

Recognizes the opportunity to explore new markets

The web is one of the fastest-growing markets in the world economy. When this is the case, a successful SEO strategy helps you find new markets and explore new economies.

Social media platforms and mobile markets can take your traffic level to a whole new level by increasing your SEO performance.

It helps you to improve your conversion rates

A website optimized for SEO is fast, easy to use, compatible with mobile and tablet devices. These features mean better conversions at the same time, which means that visitors to your website are more likely to be customers, subscribers, or loyal visitors.

Allows you to develop brand awareness with better rankings

One of the hidden advantages of being at the top of the SERPs is brand awareness. Websites that come first when users search for a term on the Internet are always more reliable for them.

Small businesses that need to build brand awareness (for local purposes or to expand nationally) need to invest in SEO and be at the top of the list for terms related to their work. Search engines play a very important role in the creation or destruction of a brand.

Recognizes the opportunity to create a special fan base with e-mail marketing

A good SEO study is a great way to create a special fan base through more traffic and email marketing. E-mail marketing is a source of traffic and revenue that existed before social media and is still very important. Many successful bloggers claim that most of their earnings come from email lists.

As you work on your SEO, make it easy for users to subscribe to your newsletter. This is a great way to get the most out of your SEO investment.

SEO is very important for your social media campaigns.

A high-ranking website will be more visible on social media because the relationship between social media and SEO is two-way. Social media popularity is good for SEO purposes, and SEO offers more social media visibility.

Simply put, when you are at the forefront of search engine search results, your interactions and conversions from social media are higher than for a page that doesn't have a good ranking.

And this is the reason; most of the businesses and website owners will try to manipulate the search results so that their site shows up higher on the search results page (SERP) than their competitors.

HOW DO SEARCH ENGINE WORK?

Search engines such as Google use an algorithm or set of rules to determine what pages to show for any given query. These algorithms have evolved to be extremely complex, and take into account hundreds or even thousands of different ranking factors to determining the rankings of their SERPs. However, there are three core metrics that search engines evaluate to determine the quality of a site and how it should rank:

Indexing

An index is a database that contains a copy of the content. Therefore, the process of entering it into the search engine database is called indexing. In addition to "indexing", the names "crawling" or "creeping" is also popular, which are mainly associated with the visualization of the process.

To better imagine the demand in the global network, we can compare it with the network of public transport stops. Each stop is a unique document (web page, PDF, JPEG, or other file types). The search engine in this case crawls all possible stops around the city.

The path you follow is the links. This network is the structure that connects all the pages. At this stage, the automated search engine robots (also called bots or spiders) are included. They aim to crawl and "crawl" through the billions of interconnected documents on the Internet. When they do, they decrypt their codes and store only selected pieces of this huge database. At a later stage, when needed and there is a search query, they will be removed.

It is not easy to save billions of pages that need to be accessible in just a split second. That's why search engine companies have built data centers around the world where thousands of machines process vast amounts of information.

Ranking

This important step is related to the interaction with the users. At this point, search engines provide them with a list of pages that are closest to their search. If in the first step we visualized subway stations, then here we can simply imagine the search engines as machines that give answers.

When a person searches for something on the Internet, the search engine digs up billions of documents. When she finds relevant content, she offers him two things: on the one hand - results that are close to what he said, and on the other - ranking these results according to the popularity of websites.

HOW CAN IMPROVE SEARCH ENGINE OPTIMIZATION?

Understanding how search engines work is only the first step of the process in improving a site's search rankings. Improving a site's rank involves leveraging various SEO techniques to optimize the site for search:

SEO optimization is done for certain keywords or phrases. These are the phrases that you want your site to be at the top of Google. A certain number of pages appear for each phrase. The more pages come out, the more competition there is. In low competition SEO optimization is easy, and in high competition to do SEO optimization requires investments of hundreds of thousands.

For example, for the keyword phrase "smoke hatch" there are about 60 results in Google and the task of optimization is easy. While for the keyword "joinery" there are about 4 million results and SEO optimization will require a lot of work.

SEO optimization requires a lot of time to achieve results, usually for several months. But on the other hand, the results are also long-lasting.
There are two main types of SEO optimization:

- Work on the site itself called On-page optimization
- Work on creating links - links to the site - called Off-page optimization

The most important thing for On-page optimization

On-page optimization means that you work on-page, ie. within your site.
The most important thing for both On-page and Off-page optimization is the creation of useful content. You need to post materials that are not found elsewhere on the Internet and are useful to people who visit your site. These materials are called unique content. The more useful materials you post on your site, the better your site ranks in search engines.

Here are some important tips for On-page Optimization:

- Post the most useful information on the site
- Post new material over some time
- Put the key phrases in the titles of the articles
- Put the key phrases in the page titles
- The number of keywords should be between 2 and 5% of the total number of words
- Do not post so many links to external sites
- Make keywords in bold
- Put buttons for links to social networks such as Facebook, Twitter, etc.

Apart from these simple rules, there are a huge number of other factors that you can take into account if you are a professional SEO optimist or using the services of SEO specialists.

The most important thing for off-page optimization

Off-page optimization means that you work outside of your site. This job is to create links from other sites to yours. The more links you create from reputable sites to your site, the better your site ranks in search engines.

Here again, the most important thing is to be able to create useful texts related to the topic of your site. Then you need to publish them on other sites. Put a link to your site in each post.

Here are some important tips for off-page optimization:

- Publish useful articles in article directories
- Create a blog and post materials with links to your site
- Arrange with your partners and friends to put links to your site
- In the text of the links put the keywords you want to optimize
- If you want to do SEO optimization for highly competitive words on Google, you need to anticipate some investment and contact a professional SEO optimization company.

BEST SEO TOOLS

As a fairly technical discipline, there are many tools and software that SEOs rely on to help with optimizing websites. Below are some commonly used free and paid tools:

Google Search Console - Google Search Console (formerly known as "Google Webmaster Tools") is a free tool provided by Google and is a standard tool in the SEO's toolkit. GSC provides rankings and traffic reports for top keywords and pages and can help identify and fix on-site technical issues.

Google Ads Keyword Planner - Keyword Planner is another free tool provided by Google, as part of their Google Ads product. Even though it is designed for paid search, it can be a great tool to use for SEO since it provides keyword suggestions and keyword search volume, which can be helpful when doing keyword research.

Backlink Analysis Tools - There are several link analysis tools out there, the two primary ones being AHREFs and Majestic. Backlink analysis tools allow users to analyze which websites are linking to their website, or the websites of competitors, and can be used to find new links during link building.

SEO Platforms - Many different SEO platforms bring together many of the tools that SEOs need to optimize sites. Some of the most popular include Moz, BrightEdge, Searchmetrics, and Linkdex. These platforms track keyword rankings, help with keyword research, identify on-page and off-page SEO opportunities, and many other tasks related to SEO.

Social Media - Most social media sites don't have a direct impact on SEO, but they can be a good tool for networking with other webmasters and building relationships that can lead to link building and guest posting opportunities.

MODULE 2
SEARCH ENGINE MARKETING

WHAT IS SEARCH ENGINE MARKETING?

A form of online marketing that increases the visibility of a website in the search engine by indexing and purchasing advertising as well as optimizing the site.

Search engine marketing (SEM) is the use of paid ads to make your site appear on the SERP pages of Google, Bing, and other search engines. The search engines use an auction system where site owners can bid on keywords that can be used as search terms by search engine users when searching for information, products, or services. This paid advertising service is Google's biggest source of revenue and can be a great way for a new business to gain momentum since the paid results will appear in prominent positions in the SERP results.

The ads are known in the digital marketing industry as pay-per-click (PPC) ads since the person posting the ad does not have to pay for it before a user clicks on the ad. There are several different formats for these PPC ads. They can be small and text-based, or larger visuals, or even video ads.

WHAT IS GOOGLE ADWORDS?

Google Ads is a smart way to reach new potential customers as they actively search for products and / or services you offer. Ads come under the term Search Engine Marketing (SEM). Google Ads is Google's keyword advertising system, but it is also possible to advertise in the same way in Microsoft's Bing search engine. Both systems are roughly the same.

Users today do a lot of preparation before contacting potential suppliers both in terms of consumer purchases (B2C) and when seeking a business partner in B2B (B2B). When in the investigation phase, a search is used actively. Then it is important that you are visible and communicated why they should choose your products or services.

PPC MARKETING

What is PPC or Pay Per Click marketing?

We will discuss the Topic PPC of Search Engine marketing i.e. Pay Per Click. Search Engine Optimization is a Free Organic Result but PPC is a Paid Advertisement. So let's know what PPC is?

Suppose any of your ads are showing in Google, if a user clicks on your ad, then you will have to pay for that click. For example, I searched in Google for Best Hotels in Amsterdam, so this is where Ad has written, it is showing the results of Google PPC. Big companies use Google PPC to sell their services, products.

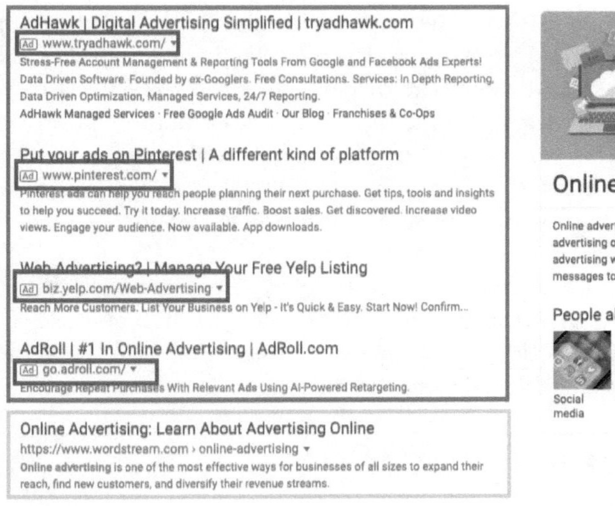

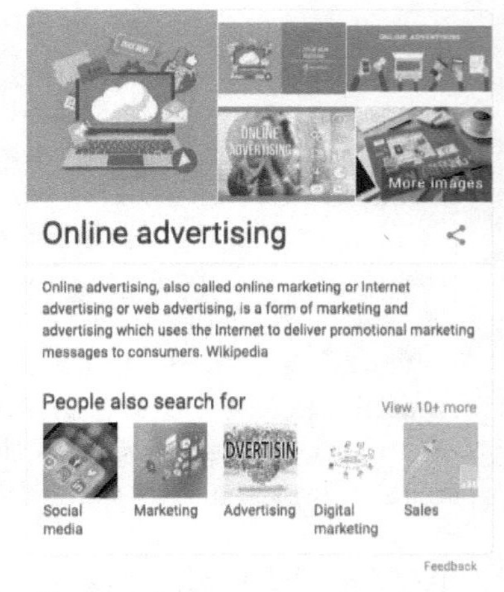

Importance and benefits of PPC:

- **Provide Fast Results:** If you have created a website today even if its SEO is not done, then by using Google PPC, you can rank your website on Google's first page means PPC provides Fast Results.

- **Cheaper than Traditional Marketing:** PPC is about 90% cheaper than Traditional Marketing because nowadays it is the era of the Internet and there are many websites on the Internet where there is a lot of traffic and you can get your ads to be shown on those websites. You can sell your products or services.

- **Independent from Google Algorithm Changes:** There are some changes in Google Algorithm from time to time, due to which the ranking of the websites keeps decreasing or increasing but it does not have any effect on PPC.

- **Reach the Right Audience:** You can target your Desired Audience with PPC, and you can sell your products and services to them, with PPC you can also target a Particular Location means you can use keywords, Location, Website, Device according to your own, Time and Date Target.

- **Budget Friendly:** You do not have to spend millions of Dollars to put PPC on your ads, but you can start your business by applying PPC on a low budget too.

How to set a PPC Campaign?

Selecting the Right PPC Keywords

- **Brand keywords:** These are keywords that include your brand name. Brand keywords are a no-brainer; they tend to have very low costs and very high-Quality Scores. Also, they yield excellent results in terms of click-through rate (CTR) and conversion rate.
- **Commercial keywords:** Commercial keywords are the most valuable terms in your PPC arsenal. These high-intent terms are generally used by prospects who are closest to the "bottom of the funnel" and most likely to buy.
- **Broader, low-intent keywords:** To expand your account and your business's reach, it's important to also bid on some broader PPC keywords that have low intent, but help you increase brand awareness. You can increase your conversion rate on broad keywords through remarketing strategies.
- **Long-tail keywords:** Long-tail keywords are the longer, highly specific, unique phrases that are often very low-cost and have less keyword competition. However, long-tail keywords often have low volume and limited impressions too.
- **Competitive keywords:** It's a good idea to allocate some budget toward competitive keywords. This allows you to get your brand and

offerings in front of people who are searching for your competitors' products or services.

TARGETED COPY

Effective ad copy can be key in keeping your pay per click advertising budget on track. When your copy addresses a targeted audience, the result is likely to be a decrease in the number of clicks but an increase in the quality of clicks. This means that click costs will go down while conversions by more qualified visitors will go up. Another way to target qualified users: make sure your PPC ad specifies what action you want them to take when they reach your site – be it to buy a product, register for a seminar, or download a file. Surprising the visitor with an unexpected request is likely to harm your pay per click marketing results.

LANDING PAGES

Keywords and copy may lead a horse to water, but PPC advertising landing pages are designed to make it drink. When visitors arrive at a landing page that supports the specific content of your PPC advertisement, consumer confidence – in your product and your brand -- soars. Customized pay per click landing pages gives customers what they need without the hassle of going through your home page. This enhanced user experience typically leads to increased sales conversion and return on investment for your pay per click marketing campaign.

WEBSITE ANALYSIS

What happens after the click-through, when users arrive at your website or landing page? Only website analysis can answer that question. By using software that analyzes your PPC advertising visitors' activity on your site, you can identify problem areas and resolve issues that may be causing you to lose pay per click conversions.

PPC advertising requires a dynamic, cohesive strategy that helps your online business connect with and convert qualified visitors in a swift, targeted manner. By giving careful consideration to the five key components of a successful pay per click marketing, you can create a PPC advertising campaign that clicks with your business' online goals.

DISPLAY ADVERTIZING

When we advertise our business or blog or website on digital media (mobile, computer, and internet) on social media, it is called digital advertising. In this way, digital marketing is the only way to make your product accessible to people in the global market through online internet, in which you can promote your product or brand   globally through digital equipment like mobile and computer. Its main objective is to reach as many people as possible. Through digital advertising, you can reach the global market at a low cost.

BID MANAGEMENT

Bid management involves the automated management of bidding for digital marketing campaigns. Bid management tools, also called bid optimization platforms, enable you to automate your CPC (cost-per-click) bids for different campaigns.

Today, the term "bid management" is also used to manage bids in the display ad market, with the development of real-time bidding. This automated management is possible, thanks to algorithms defined by the marketing manager based on the set objectives and available resources. By using a digital analytics solution with a bid management tool, you can generate profits as well as brand awareness.

TOP SEM TOOLS

Google Adwords Keyword Tool- It is a free Google keyword tool that can help you find the density of keywords and the number of users who search for things by using these keywords monthly all over the globe in certain countries. But this software is not very convenient for generating long-tail keywords and it shows the same results to everyone. That is why your Google keyword research is not very competitive. If you are new to website business, it would be good for you to learn about META Tags (a META Tag is a piece of text written in the HEAD of your HTML page) and realize that they play an important role in getting a good keyword ranking. To generate the right META Tag we advise you to use a great SEO tool:

META Tag Generator- Once you have the website title, description, and keywords, you will be able to generate a META Tag that is right for your page. Many search engines pay attention to them and use them for indexing sites.

Another criterion of successful website promotion on the internet is original content. Smart search engines quickly define the right owner of texts, and even if you decide to "borrow" somebody's writings, soon you will be punished. There are several tools to help you can check how original your content is. For example:

Plagspotter- This wonderful software will tell you if your content has been copied and spread throughout the internet. Simply enter a URL and get the addresses of those sites that have scrapped your texts without giving you a credit for your work. You will find information about what percentage of your content has been copied and even receive a few tips on how to make the plagiarists get rid of the stolen content.

Now, when you have corrected mistakes and optimized your web site after all the work has been done, you would like to see where your site places in the most widely-used search engine - and this is where you will need Alexa.

Alexa- Alexa calculates traffic rankings that are based on the number of users who visit a website during a single day as well as the page views. If a particular user visits the same URL several times during the same day, all those visits will be counted as one. It gathers information about the user's IPs and the pages they visit.

Header Checker Tool- You will need this tool to see which response code you will get after entering a certain URL. You must make sure that your web site's URL returns the appropriate status code and all the redirects work well. It is very important to use the correct type of redirect if you want to optimize your page.

AdSense Calculator- Do you want to know how much you can earn daily, monthly, or yearly? Do you want to know how much you are going to be paid per click? Then implement the AdSense calculator, a piece of PPC software, to your page and calculate the average CPC and find out other commercial information with its help.

SEMrush- SEMrush is a powerful keyword software with an impressive database that not only can show you the keywords according to which the website ranks and the number of searches by these keywords per month, but it can also reveal all your rival's secrets to help you to work out a better strategy and leave your opponents far behind.

MODULE 3
SOCIAL MEDIA MARKETING AND OPTIMIZATION

WHAT IS SOCIAL MEDIA MARKETING?

Social media marketing is the process of creating content to promote your business and products on various platforms such as Facebook, Instagram, and Twitter. Your unique content must be tailored to the specific platform on which it is shared to increase sales through these social channels, as well as the recognition and recognition of your brand.

ADVANTAGES OF SOCIAL MEDIA

There are various reasons why your company should use social media marketing, so we've created a list of the four most important reasons to consider.

A. Brand approval in 2019, social networks were used by more than 3.2 billion people worldwide. Precisely because of this huge number of users, you need to ensure the sharing of content for your business

related to your products, as well as details about your company through a platform or two and thus improve the visibility of your brand.
It has been proven that social media increases brand credibility by increasing engagement in social profiles.

Social engagement includes things like commenting, liking, and sharing. Social media also helps you with brand awareness by directing traffic directly to your site. You can do this by placing direct links to your website in your account, bio section, or directly in the posts.

B. Increase sales Promoting and sharing your products on social media is a simple way to improve
Attract leads, increasing conversions and sales, because you present your products and services to people who have chosen to follow your account or your page. Here are some examples of ways you can use social media to attract more customers:

- Create contests and games for your visitors and followers.
- Add links to your website and offers in the sections of your accounts.
- Host live videos to introduce a new product, review an existing one, or just share
- Create a social media marketing campaign for at least one of the channels you use.

C. By connecting and communicating with your followers on social media, you will be able to build lasting relationships between them and your business. This is achieved by communicating with them in your posts, answering their questions and comments, and providing them with any help they may need. You can also ask your followers questions about your products, their problem points, or give gifts to help you build trust and show them how much you value their input and support.

For example, someone has written a review for your product and you send them a discount code on your next purchase.

D. Learn from competitors, Social media is a great way to monitor your competitors - whether it's in terms of their social media tactics, the products they advertise, the campaigns they implement, or the level of interaction with their followers.

Social networks allow you to see what works and what doesn't work for your competition and therefore helps you decide what should or should not change in your campaign approach.

E. Finally, reviewing your competitors' social accounts can help you make sure your marketing stand out is unique to your brand.

SOCIAL MEDIA MARKETING STRETEGY

There are five steps you need to follow to make sure your social media marketing plan is sustainable and will have a positive impact on your business.

- Research the profile of your clients.
- Determine which social platforms you will sell.
- Create unique and compelling content.
- Organize a schedule for your publications.
- Analyze your impact and results.

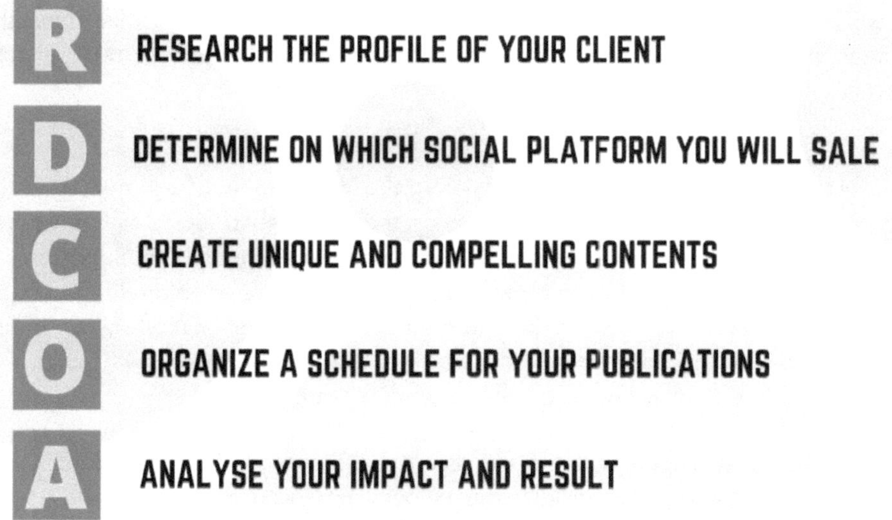

Let's cover these steps in more detail so you can start applying them in real-time.

Research the profile of your clients

The first step to creating a social media marketing strategy is to identify who your potential customers are so you can target them to their needs and interests.To do this, think about the people you are trying to reach and why and how you would classify them as a group.

For example, if your company sells sporty-elegant clothing, you can classify your target audience as "stylish," who like to wear sporty elegant clothing regularly - a style known as "sporty-elegant."

Once you've defined your buyer and audience profile, you'll be able to determine what content will attract this type of followers and the customers you hope to win, and how you can create engaging content to keep your followers interested.

Determine on which social platforms you will sell

If you are going to be involved in social media marketing, it is extremely important to choose which social networks you will share your content.

There is not necessarily a right or wrong answer when it comes to which social networks your business should use. Rather, you need to determine the target audience and where your potential customers tend to spend most of their time.

- **Snapchat:** Young people make up the largest share of 300 million users.
- **Facebook:** young people make up the largest share of 2.2 billion users.
- **Youtube:** young people make up the largest share of 1.9 billion users.
- **Twitter:** Young people make up the largest share of 335 million users.
- **Pinterest:** is used by the youngest and oldest and makes up the largest part of the 250 million users
- **Tik – Tok:** everyone in this network is young □

To choose the right platform for your specific type of business, buyers, and target audience, consider the differences between social media channels so you can make an informed decision.

Create unique and compelling content

With billions of social media users around the world, there's no doubt that at least some of your followers - or the people who view your profile - have also seen the content of your competitor or that of other businesses in your industry.

Therefore, it is essential that you build and publish content on social media that stands out and gives the user a reason to click on this important "Follow" button and interact with your brand.

Take a look at how your competitors present or advertise their products; consider whether you can present your products more uniquely.

Also, take advantage of the features offered by the platform you are using. For example, you can make live videos on Facebook, where you can share information about a product, the upcoming launch of a new product, or something related to attracting the interest of your followers.

Finally, use your current customers and promoters to help you generate content. You can do this by republishing their content or encouraging them to use the hashtag "#" to share their own experiences and photos with your products.

Schedule your posts

One of the easiest ways to ensure that your content is shared as planned is to use some kind of social media management solution or tool (automation or delayed publishing).

These tools allow you to write statuses, prepare photos and videos, and specify in advance when to publish them.

They also automatically share your content on a schedule and monitor the social engagement of the created posts.

Social media management tools save you time and allow you to focus on your other tasks. Here are some of the most popular.

- **Sprout Social**

  Sprout Social is a social media marketing and management solution designed to help your team organize and plan content creation, manage campaigns, and track engagement, accompanied by content analysis.

- **HubSpot**
  HubSpot offers a social media tool - as part of marketing software - to help you publish and track your content and build real connections with your followers. You can plan and publish your content in advance and compare in-depth reports on the engagement of your posts to understand the effectiveness of different types of content, as well as what time of day is best to post.

- **Hootsuite**

Hootsuite is a social media management platform for finding, planning, managing, and reporting your content. You can schedule posts across all your channels at once and measure ROI with comprehensive content analysis.

The best ones seem to follow (don't get mad at the big ones, but they don't do half the good work of the next tools)

Now you may be wondering how often you should post content on your social media channels.

As a rule, you should only post on social media when you have quality content to share. However, you want users to interact with it, and if they don't like it, they won't.

That is, you must have a reason to publish the content. Here's how to get the right balance when it comes to publishing frequency.

If you post too infrequently, you will be forgotten by your followers.If you post too often, you will probably become annoying to your followers. Both situations could potentially lead to the loss of followers and reduced engagement.To avoids this, there are many studies and resources available that explain the publication frequency standards that you should follow. Every business is different, so find what works for your audience.

Analyze your impact and results

One of the most important aspects of social media marketing is to ensure that your efforts are successful in helping you achieve your goals.

To determine this, you will need to follow all your posts on each channel.

You can do this by viewing and managing your social media reports.Social media metrics are data related to the success of your posts and their impact on your audience and customers across platforms. These metrics can include data on engagement levels, likes, follow-ups, shares, and any other interactions on each platform.

Here are 10 of the most important indicators to monitor:

- **Commitment:**

This includes clicks, comments, likes, and responses to your social media posts. Depending on the type of platform, there is also a specific type of engagement such as "Saved" for Instagram and "Pinned" for Pinterest.

- **Followers:** This is the number of people you have in your account who have clicked the "Follow" button and regularly see your content in their feed.

- **Impressions:** This is how many times a post was viewed from your profile or page, whether or not someone clicked on that post. This often happens when someone scrolls in the feed but does not click on anything.

- **Video views:** on Facebook, Snapchat, Instagram, or any other social channel with video capabilities, this is the number of views each video has received.

- **Profile visits:** The number of people who opened your social media page.

- **Mentions:** This is the number of times your account was mentioned in a post by a user who is part of your audience.

- **Tags:** This is when your audience adds your company account name or hashtag to another post.

- **Repost:** This is when a member of your audience posts some of your content on their account.

- **Shares:** These are the posts that your followers and audience borrow from your account and share with their followers.

You can influence all of these metrics, increase your social presence, and improve your overall engagement in your account by using the same tactics you would use to attract leads.You can also communicate with your followers more often by talking to them, tagging them in content, answering their questions, like their posts, encouraging them to use your hashtags, and sharing your content.

MODULE 4
ON-PAGE AND OFF-PAGE OPTIMIZATION

Is the traffic on your website or blog not coming at all, even after publishing many of your posts? This means that you need to optimize the page completely to make it SEO friendly by Post Optimization. If your optimization is strong, then only through this you can easily rank the post on the first page. In this chapter, we will know what "On-Page SEO" is and how optimizations for posts do.

WHAT IS ON-PAGE SEO?

On-page SEO is the search engine optimization that optimizes the post while writing or updating the post before publishing it. Due to perfection in this, the post can easily be ranked on the first page of the search engine. Before that, we knew what SEO is and why it is important for your blog or website.

In this lesson, we will know what is On-Page and Off-page optimization and what are the variations in it. And also, in this lesson, I will show you how to apply it, how to do it. And this is important for your website and blog; I will give full information about this. With this, you can optimize the post perfectly, how to make the post search engine friendly, as well as how it can easily rank on a search engine.

ON-PAGE SEO DEFINITION

If we talk in simple language, then all the ways that we use to rank our blog on the first number of the search engine is called Search Engine Optimization. The techniques we follow while writing a post or article are called On-Page SEO. If we become a master in this, then we can easily rank every post on the first page of the search engine.

In this, we use many techniques like keyword research, post title, permalink, meta description, quality content, use of keywords in the right place, image optimization, proper use of headings, internal and external linking.

So if you want to master yourself in search engine optimization, then you have to become strong by teaching post-optimization first. The day you become an expert in this, your blog will also start coming on the first rank of search engine.

WHY DO WE USE ON-PAGE SEO?

Most of these tools are used to do keyword research. When we study a lot, after exams and after working hard day and night and go to write exams, then the result of the person who writes exams is better. The results are output and we get to know who has studied well. In the same way, even though we know everything about SEO, if we are weak in doing practical search engine optimization, then its knowledge is of no use.

The output of Title, Permalink, and Meta description can be understood in this way. And this explains the perfection of our post-optimization. Do keyword research before you start writing posts. Keyword research is very important.

Mostly these tools are used to do keyword research.

- Bing Keyword Planner
- Google Keyword Planner

DIFFERENCE BETWEEN ON-PAGE AND OFF-PAGE SEO

The method of optimization we follow while writing a post or blog is called on-page optimization. In this, we take every care in writing the article which comes inside this technique. When we do the optimization of our site outside the post, it is called **off-page optimization**. It is also considered to be a very important factor which is very important for our website and blog. Here I am going to tell you the difference between them so that you will understand them.

On-Page Optimization	Off-Page Optimization
While writing a post, it is important to optimize its title and insert the targeted keyword in it.	Understand the backlink building strategy and follow the rules in the right way and make a backlink.
Permalink should be written short and it must also contain keywords.	Social bookmarking is an important step under off page.
Use Heading 1,2,3 in the post correctly and add keywords in them.	Posting a guest in a site with a niche like yours.
Write a meta description that the visitor is interested in reading and must read the post openly.	Directory submission.
Use keywords in the first paragraph and last paragraph.	To be active in social media websites like Facebook, Twitter, Instagram to give signal to Google.
Keyword density has to be kept, that is, not more than 2.5%.	Forum submission
The keyboard has to be used in the Alt Tag of the image.	Blog commenting
Internal and external linking is very important.	Staying active in discussion websites like sharing your links in Quora and clearing up people's queries.

ON-PAGE SEO STRETEGIES TO RANK IN SEO

Post Title

In this, the post title is the most important role. By properly using keywords in the post title, we optimize our posts perfectly for search engines. Under this, the post title is a very important factor.

In this screenshot, you can easily understand how our output will look when we have a fully optimized Post title, Permalink, and Meta description.

Write post title and use keywords in our post title, search engine should be optimized. For this, I am giving you some tips so that you can write keywords in your title perfectly.

- **Keyword Placement:** Put Targeting Keyword (i.e. post related keyword, the keyword with which you want to rank your post) at the beginning of your post title. Try to start "Post Title" with keywords only. I agree that we cannot begin the title of every post with keywords, sometimes it does not even fit. But try to make sure that the targeted keyword is not in the last title of the post title.

- **Use Effective Words:** Use these words to make the post title more SEO friendly. Such as Effective, Most, Important, Best, Top, Strategies, Surprising, Essential, Ultimate guide, Beginners guide, Complete guide can be used to create titles and attributes using these words.

- **Use Of Numerics:** It is easy to attract people by adding numbers to the title. They quickly read such posts
Example:
10 effective methods
5 Best Plugins
10 Mistakes we should avoid etc.

- **Avoid Repetition of keyword:** Use the keyword only once in the title of the post. Do not put it more than once. Keyword repetition represents negative optimization.

Permalink

Like Title, Permalink for posts is also important for On-Page. We also need to add focus keywords in the permalink. Apart from this, I am telling you some tips to follow him.

- **Short URL:** Permalink should be kept short. And along with this, you must put your focus keyword or main keyword in it.
  Permalink should keep us short and with this, we must put our focus keyword or I keyword in it.

- **Delete Useless Permalink**Delete the useless URL manually and enter the search engine friendly URL
  When we write the title of extra length, permalink automatically becomes "xyz.com/?p=101" like this. So never use this type of permalink. Change it yourself, follow the process in the same manner as I am telling you here.

- **Never Use Stop Words**
  Stop words like "a", "the", "on", "and" are called. Never use these words in Permalink, and then it is better for SEO.

Meta Description

It says no first impression is the last impression. Our Meta Description also does the same thing. According to the search engine, the important factor after Title and Permalink is Meta Description. It is important to use the Meta Description well because we can also rank our page easily. We should write an SEO Optimized Meta Description to convince our readers that the information they are searching for is available in this post.

According to Google, 320 words long description was allowed until a few months back. But right now the length of the description should be between 150-170 words. Make sure to use keywords in the description of your post.

Keywords Density inside Content

We should use more density keywords in the first paragraph of our content. Be sure to include keywords within the first 100-150 words of content in good density. Keyword research is done so that we can get good organic traffic from the search engine. Along with this, the selection of keywords is done keeping the CPC in mind. Using keywords within content properly allows search engines to know what content is written about. And in this way, our post in the search engine is well optimized.

Proper Use of Heading and Sub-heading With Keywords

We can use Headings to get better results. We can strengthen our optimization technique using proper H2, H3, H4 heading. Do not repeat the headings. Never use H1 heading inside your post. Because already the title of our post is H1 Heading.Also, put your focus keyword in Heading, it is very effective for our post. But keep in mind that use focus keywords in less than 50% headings.

Image Optimization

We use images to attract visitors. In the image, we can disassemble the topic of our post without writing it. Visitors understand from the perfectly optimized image that they will get the information they want here.

The thing to keep in mind is that while designing the image, it is important to follow some factories as well. Using these factors, we can make our image 100% SEO optimized and user friendly. SEO Friendly Image makes our On-page very strong.

1. **Image Title:** Use the keyword in the title of the image used within the post. This has the advantage that the search engine recognizes the keywords from the title of our image and helps to rank our posts.

Do not use unknown titles in the image title, but remove them

- **ALT Tag:** Writing alt tag along with image title also makes our post search engine friendly. Most important must add their focus keyword to it.

- **Image Size:** Image size proves to be an important factor for our post-optimization. We always use images in our posts. Image size must be at least. This will not take much time to load the blog page.
- **Featured Image:** To give user-friendly experience to your readers, create a featured image in your post. The image that we use as Thumbnail is called the featured image.

Use Outbound and Internal Links

Use external and internal links as needed to optimize your post and SEO friendly. When we add a link to another website in our post, then they add an external link and link to their blog post, it is called an internal link. When we add a link to another blog or website in our post, in this way we give them a backlink, which proves very helpful for their SEO. Also, our own experience is strong.

- **Internal Links:** To increase user engagement, we use internal linking. With internal linking, we show the user that if you have come here in search of a fruit mango, then you have all the fruits apple, banana, orange, etc. Will be found here

  With this, we can make full use of the quality of our content and engage the user in other pages from the landing page. Suppose traffic is too much in one of your posts, you can get traffic by adding a link to other posts from that post. But remember to add related posts as internal links.

1. **External Linking:** When we add another website in our post, it is called external linking. Suppose in our post that we are writing about a feature of Youtube and for some information, information is provided in the YouTube Help Forum, then we can add a link to it in our post.

This is SEO friendly; there is no problem with this. Rather, it increases our search engine ranking.

Detailed Content Post

In today's time, it is better than wasting time on backlinks to spend that time in creating content because if your content fully helps your reader and gives him complete information, then nothing can help you rank better than this can. This means that good content will rank even without backlinks.

Write the as long post as possible to rank on the first page in Google search results. Nowadays, there are many bloggers whose posts are of 2000 words and their content quality is also good. So now you can understand.

If you want to get a good rank on the first page of Google, then you have to write every post more than 2000 words as well as keep the content quality also excellent. But if you can't write that much then try to make sure at least 1000 words. Chances of coming to the first page due to it will be less.

Also, the higher the content length, the more you can keep the density of keywords. Density is to be kept below 2.5%, but your keywords will be used more often. This will make Google as easy to understand the topic as to what it is about. In this way, the chance of getting a higher ranking in search results will be more.

Page Loading Speed

Google checks every blog post before ranking it in its search results. Page speed is also an important factor for SEO friendly blogs. Also, under post-optimization, it is a very important factor. If the page loading speed is good then google bots index the post quickly. Good loading speed is important for a better user experience. Google does not rank

Use Social Sharing Buttons

If the quality of our content is good, then our readers will share it everywhere through the social sharing button. Despite not having the option of sharing, no one will share it.

We can increase our page views by using social sharing. When visitors coming from social sites spend time on our page, then Google gets a positive signal in away. WordPress users can easily enable such sharing buttons by installing social sharing plugins.

Use of related informative video

Nowadays people are more attracted than text content as well as media contents. So we should also add well-optimized images and videos to the text content. If you use Google Analytics, then you will know about the Bounce Rate and Time on-page.

- **Bounce rate:** When a visitor comes to the landing page of our blog and goes back without visiting another page, it is called the Bounce rate.
- **Time On-Page:** Time on page is spoken by a visitor who stays on our blog.

By inserting video content, we can stop the readers on our page for some time, this reduces the bounce rate and also increases the time duration, which increases our search ranking.Any video you add to your post, should be a video conversion of the same topic. So that the user has a better experience and they will spend more time in the post.

Google also notices every little thing and gives importance to them. That is why it is very important to write SEO friendly posts as well as the longer the visitors stop on the page, the better the ranking will be.

MODULE 5
CONTENT MARKETING

WHAT IS CONTENT MARKETING?

Today the world is becoming completely digital. In which many kinds of work are being done, such as digital marketing which is now being done a lot. Talking about content marketing, it is also a part of digital marketing. If you also want to do content marketing, then in today's post, you will explain in detail, what content marketing is.

Content marketing is a method where Valuable Content is created. It is shared by users who need it and then promoted by social media, online media, print media, or television. Before knowing about content marketing, it becomes even easier if you know that what do mean by "content".

WHAT IS CONTENT?

Content means that which is used as text, video, or image in a website or newspaper. They are used to attract users. These are presented to the users by adopting a professional approach for some purpose such as to identify their product to the user, to guide or inform the users through the content, by writing an article and presenting it to the user, it is called content.

TYPES OF CONTENTS

- **Infographics**

  In infographics, the text is placed over the image. It is the Banner and Logo in Shops, TV Advertisement which is called Symbol of its product or company which gives information about that product. It is a Vertical Graphics in which Charts, Graphs, Statistics as well as more information are written.

- **Videos**

Marketing through video is very attractive. It also attracts more than text. If video clips are added to the content, then the user is easy to understand.

- **Text**

  It is a core part of Content Marketing. The user can be further attracted by writing great content. Write good content about your product. Text, poetry, paragraphs can be written in text content.

- **Webpages**

  If the web pages are well created or written in Content Marketing Web Pages and SEO optimized in a better way, then this will attract users to your content.

- **Images**

  If the image is used for marketing the content, it makes the user easy to understand. The information of the image product is well explained to the users.

IMPORTANCE OF CONTENT MARKETING

The way digital marketing is expanding. Looking at it, it seems that in the coming time it will become even more important. So if you are in the business of digital marketing then it is incomplete without content marketing. Success can be achieved only through Content Marketing.

WHAT IS CONTENT MARKETING STRETEGY?

If you do any work in advance if you do not plan it properly then even better results are not possible. So for good results, Content Marketing Strategy will also have to be made.

- First, you have to understand your mission.
- After this install your Key Performance Indicators.
- Now you have to know your audience how they will have to make content according to the content they like.
- After this, the type of content is to determine what kind of content you need.
- Now create and publish your content.

- Focus on promoting your business and product according to the user's choice.

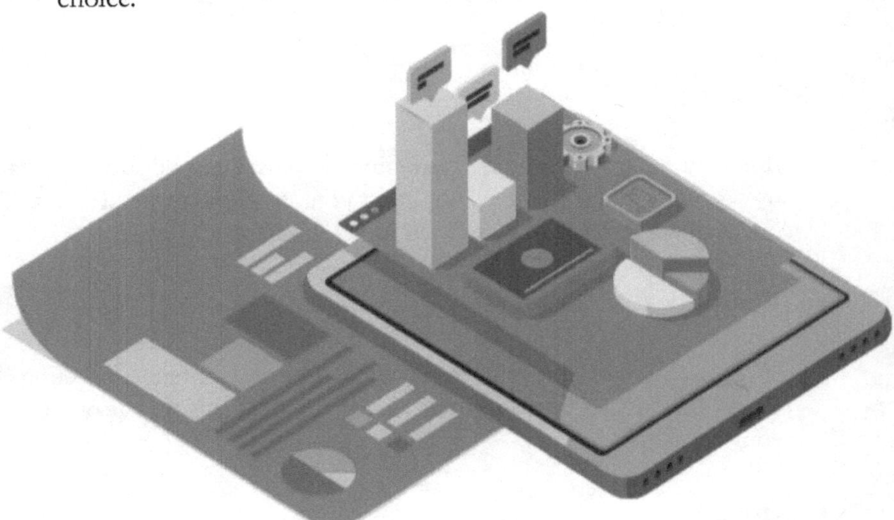

BENEFITS OF CONTENT MARKETING STRETEGY

- If you work on Content Marketing Strategy, then you also get its benefits. Know about the Benefits Of Marketing Strategy.
- This will make the user trust your brand and they will be honest about your product and your brand reputation will also increase.
- If your content is effective then it increases your site traffic.
- It increases social traffic and followers.
- Content helps to be listed at the top in search engines.
- If you put good content on your site, the user's trust in your site will increase and if your site gets an inbound link from other sources, it increases the domain authority of the website. The higher the domain authority, the better the search ranking.
- When you increase the content on the website, the rank of your website in the search engine will increase and your website will appear at the top in the search engine, then users will open your website first.
- More and more Backlinks are available.

Slow loading blog posts well in search results. You can use speed increase plugins. Use a minimum of content on the homepage such as widgets, posts, links, and images. Keep the size of the images optimized so that the image size is reduced and fast loading is done.

The template or theme of the blog should be written using minimum codes and be responsive and fast loading. Research has found that the blog or website whose loading time is less than 3-4 seconds, the visitors stop immediately and go to another site.

So if your blog speed is low then this is a serious matter. Solve it quickly.

MODULE 6
E-MAIL MARKETING

WHAT IS E-MAIL MARKETING?

When we hear the term email marketing, our brains don't feel generating another word - spam, right?

But we don't want to talk about email stacks that bombard email inboxes, we don't want to teach or digest tips on how to send as many emails as possible that can annoy your users. Nor do we want you to blindly take any action just because others are doing it and do it without any clear tactics, and worst of all without seeing the results or knowing how to analyze them.

We want to talk about the real benefits of email marketing, its effective and correct use, and what the statistics say and why you shouldn't exclude this action from your online marketing strategy.

THE BENEFITS OF E-MAIL MARKETING

Targeted Marketing

If the available or accumulated database is properly segmented, your marketing message using appropriately prepared e-mails is much more targeted and much targeted to the target audience of users.

Brand Awareess

Properly created and responsibly used email sequences increase brand awareness and increase its authority.

Analysis of results

With professional email marketing tools, you can accurately measure the effectiveness of your campaigns and continuously track results, and respond and change tactical actions accordingly.

Saving time, money and effort

By pre-planning and choosing the right tools, you can simultaneously reach a large amount of your target audience in a much shorter amount of time, at a much lower cost, and with accurate knowledge of their reaction to plan their next steps to influence their behavior and influence their decisions.

Dissemination of information

Relevant information sent by e-mail can be easily disseminated among users with the click of a "forward" button.

Effective communication

Email marketing is a way to reach your current and future customers more often, closer, and in real-time. Your email sequences can be automated, scheduled in advance, and run when you're not even at your workplace.

Method of market research

A tailor-made email campaign can also be a great tool to explore the needs of your target audience, try a much larger marketing campaign, conduct surveys, surveys, and get quick and easy feedback on services already provided and products sold.

And here are just some benefits, and the list could go on, but we want to talk more about what the phrases we use mean - correctly, effectively, purposefully, etc. Let's start from the beginning - the database and its segmentation. If you already have a database or are using various registration forms to compile a database, be sure to segment it.

THINGS TO REMMEBER

- If you provide services to the B2B segment and your database consists of companies from different Lithuanian cities, their type of activity differs, their size, they have purchased or were interested in different services - do not send general letters to everyone!

- Divide your database into individual segments depending on what exactly service you can offer based on the company's operations, its size, or even the city in which it operates.

- If your segment is B2C, the rule remains the same - divide the recipients into smaller groups as much as possible, by demographics, by interests, or by the different products you can offer.

- The second very important thing is the tools you use in your email campaigns and how they help you see the effectiveness of your campaigns.

- If you are sending emails en masse with the help of your server - stop doing so! You lose very useful statistics, and you also can't make your job easier with automated email systems. (Tools recommendation for what you can choose as your online marketing satellite for email campaigns - Mailchimp, ActiveCampaign, Ontraport).

- When it comes to segmenting data based on available recipient information, the next step is to use professional tools to gather even more useful statistics about the behavior of your existing and potential customers, respond accordingly, and take action to increase your conversions.

- By having as much information as possible, you create a significant advantage over your competitors because you know how the market reacts; the information allows you to have easier access to consumers, making your offer much more subtle and targeted.

- Summarizing all the advantages and correct actions, this way you create your own online marketing action strategy that saves you time, energy, costs. With an accurate plan that you can follow and respond to your consumer behavior with the help of professional tools, you create a competitive advantage for yourself and have much higher conversions that generate double the return on investment.

So if you haven't used any email marketing tool yet or tested yourself in this field, the next time you hear the phrase email marketing - don't be skeptical, this method won't promise to retire anywhere for a long time, just ask what will be popular and recognize, because it will do everything correctly, and whose information will remain in the spam boxes.

MODULE 7
MOBILE MARKETING

WHAT IS MOBILE MARKETING?

People love their smartphones An estimated 83% of American adults own a cell phone, and 42% have an iPhone or smartphone, according to a recent report from the Pew Internet Project.

The study also found that 87% of smartphone users access the internet or email from their device. The fact is that thanks to the explosion of mobile devices enabled for the internet, entrepreneurs and their customers can communicate anywhere. That's why mobile marketing or mobile marketing is so important for a business, which consists of a set of methods and formats to promote products and services, which use mobile devices as a communication tool.

Take advantage of mobile marketing to advertise your business. There was a time when email marketing was very important to merchants. It has changed the face of conventional marketing and the way companies view this aspect of a business. Now, with the advent of smart mobile devices with much greater connectivity, mobile marketing is far beyond email marketing.

Mobile marketing gives the user advantages such as low cost, personalization, and easy tracking, thus reducing the workforce, while giving the entrepreneur better business benefits and profits. Like everything else, mobile marketing also has its drawbacks and shortcomings.

ADVANTAGES OF MOBILE MARKETING

Mobile marketing offers a large number of business professionals.

- Consumers always carry their mobile phones with them. Most of the time, users have mobile phones, which means that they receive messages the moment they are sent. Even if the phone is in standby mode, the message is received as soon as the user turns on their mobile device. This makes mobile marketing techniques almost instantaneous.

- Creating content for mobile devices, whether text, images, or video, is easier and cheaper than creating content for desktops and laptops.

- The mobile medium facilitates the issuance of promotions and services to stimulate consumer marketing. Besides, users can store virtual information on the phone and carry it until they need to use it.

- Because the screen size of a mobile phone is small, it limits the range of content that can be displayed. This makes it convenient for content creators who can keep it basic and simple. Also, easier content adapts easily to different mobile platforms.

- The mobile platform interacts directly with the users of their mobile phones. This allows for personalized interaction to a large extent. Taking advantage of this, marketers can engage in direct dialogue with the consumer by receiving immediate feedback via text messages.

- The user's response can be tracked almost instantly. This helps the mobile merchant to better understand and analyze consumer behavior, thus improving their standards of service.

- Mobile content can be easily shared between users, so mobile marketing can have huge viral benefits. Consumers invariably share good information and offer with their friends and family, so companies get much more exposure without extra effort.

- Most people own mobile phones rather than desktops or laptops, which means that mobile marketing reaches a far wider and more diverse audience, especially in remote regions of the world. Mobile marketing also gives the entrepreneur the advantage of geographic location and sending location-specific messages to users using GPS and Bluetooth technology.

- Mobile marketing is still evolving, so the niche is convenient for any new merchant.

- Mobile users are increasingly using microblogging platforms like Twitter from their mobile phones. This microblogging feature can be very useful for a marketer.

- Mobile payment is convenient for consumers. They offer a secure online payment environment that works through modern mobile web systems.

As a result, consumers do not need physical currency to make a mobile purchase or pay an online bill.

In short, the advantages of mobile marketing are:

- Immediate results
- Convenience
- Direct marketing
- Easy tracking
- Viral potential
- Mass communication is easy
- The niche is not saturated
- Microblogging benefits
- Mobile payment

DISADVANTAGES OF MOBILE MARKETING

There are several findings related to mobile marketing. They include:

- Mobile devices do not have a special standard, unlike computers and laptops. Mobile phones come in many shapes and sizes, so the screen size is not constant. Mobile platforms differ significantly from each other, using different operating systems and browsers. Creating a single campaign for all of them can be difficult.

- Mobile bookmarks need to receive and respect the fact that users protect their privacy online. They should only engage in promotional activities if they have permission from the user.

- The mobile phone usually comes with a small screen and no mouse. This means that navigating a mobile phone is difficult for the user, even if there is a touch screen. As a result, the ads may remain intact, as the user may find it too annoying to examine each of them in detail

Briefly, the disadvantages of mobile marketing are as follows:

- The platforms are too diverse
- Confidentiality
- Mobile phone navigation complications

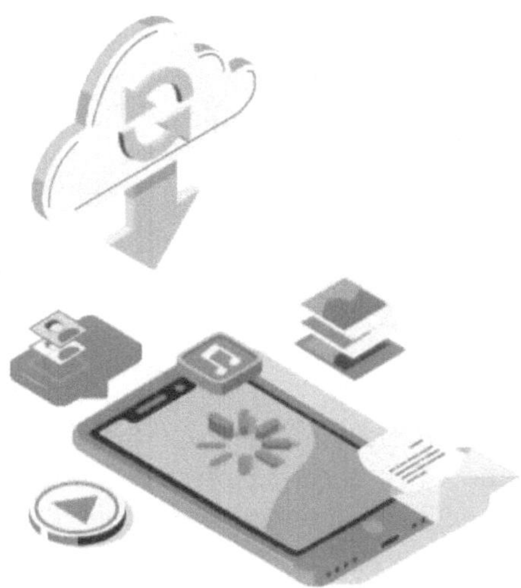

MOBILE MARKETING STRATEGIES

You can use these strategies to capture customers from mobile devices through the mobile marketing that are favorable to the customer interaction:

Responsive design

The enterprise must offer a design that can adapt to the screen on which it is navigating, whether PC, mobile, or tablets. The page should load quickly and allow all information to be accessed with a few clicks.

Presentation campaigns

While headphones with large screens larger than 5 inches are being installed, it must be taken into account that the space for online advertising is reduced, for this reason; the design of the Show is always important, including valuing two key features; shortening and impact

Custom Messages

Messages should be brief and concise, but overwhelming. This means that they should get the customer's attention, be as personal as possible, and offer the customer those products or services that you may be interested in. On the other hand, the articles for mobile marketing need to have a dramatic headline and the most interesting information must be presented at the beginning, this way the client's attention will be captured and you will want to share.

Geolocation

According to adviser Luth Research and SoundBite Communications, 86% of smartphone users use these devices to find a location, services, and tablets near the area where they are located. So the Marketing Is Nearly Fundamental to Local Businesses and so advertising in places like Google Adwords o Place-based Social Ads, it will be necessary to earn close customers.

Videos

This is one of the most widely consumed formats via smartphones that are seen in most social networks, such as Instagram from YouTube. Moreover, as a form of ad, it gains more strength and engagement among the audience.

MODULE 8
AFFILIATE MARKETING

WHAT IS AFFILIATE MARKTING?

Have you ever dreamed of waking up in the morning, opening your laptop, and finding out that you had made money while you slept? I do this through affiliate marketing. Yes, this is called passive income over time.

Affiliate marketing is like farming. You cannot reap what you sow. It takes time to grow, but if you do it right and consistently, you will see results. Affiliate marketing is one of the most effective ways to make money online.

The main idea of affiliate marketing is to promote other people's products, and if any person buying something that you're promoting, you get a commission. Affiliate marketing is a great business model and it is a different situation for everyone. As a business, they want to sell more products and they will be happy to pay you to bring your customers.

Now, as a customer, they will be able to decide the information before buying a product that you appreciate. You don't have your product to make money. Only by promoting a product that you think is valuable to your audience can you start earning money through advertising marketing.

Affiliate marketing is a collaborative effort. Everyone's contribution to the work is included. Advertisers need to advertise their products. Publishers need to have promotional products. The user requires the publisher to search for the product. Of course, without a client, both the advertiser and the publisher will not pay.

Let's take a closer look at each role.

Advertisers - Often referred to as sellers, creators, brands, retailers, and retailers. An advertiser is usually the person who creates a product. These can be small private businesses or multimillion-dollar corporations.

Publisher - Often referred to as an affiliate marketer. Partner marketers can work individually or in groups. The publisher may advertise a single or multiple products (recommended - do not place all your eggs in one basket. You must have multiple revenue streams). Their work is to give the audience enough value so that they can buy from advertisers.

Customer - Also known as a customer. Customers are what make every corner of the globe. Without users, both publishers and advertisers will be unlucky. No sales = No commission.

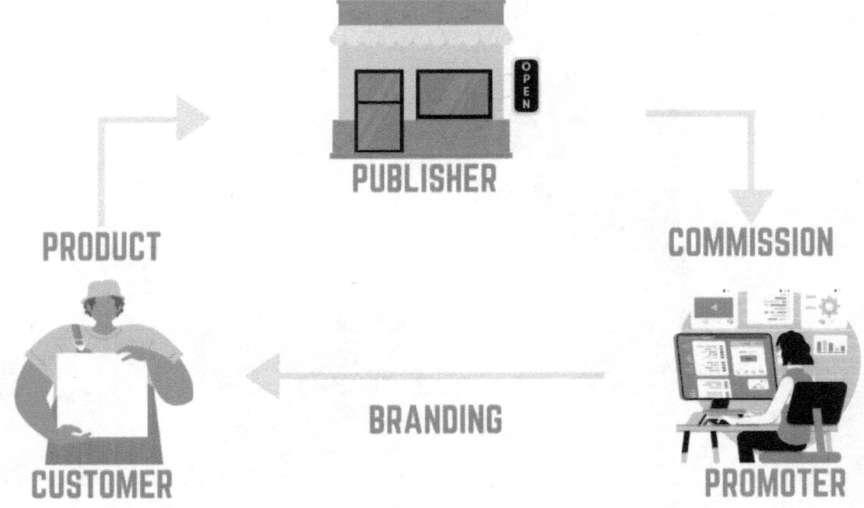

Now it's time to market these users through channels that connect them to publishers.Whether it depends on the product's review on the blog or YouTube.

When it comes to affiliate marketing, I can't say enough about why we need to be completely transparent and fair. Don't advertise a product just because you make good money.

If you can find a product, that is valuable to your audience, explain their strengths and weaknesses, and how you can help them with their needs. If they think this product is valuable, they will buy it.

In affiliate marketing, your job is to find products that your audience thinks are valuable. The most common places to find these products are through individual companies (affiliate programs) or a network of affiliate programs.

For most beginners, they start as human Amazon Associates because they have millions of different products that can fit a large number of bodies. However, the salary is not so high, but if done correctly, you will be able to live properly.
However, if you are in the digital marketing space, it is better to search for products through the network.

An affiliate network is an intermediary between a publisher and an advertiser. An advertiser or product developer can advertise their digital products online through ClickBank, which will handle payments and product delivery.

Affiliate networks will take stock, but it is easier to manage all payments and product delivery by hand.

Another reason why many advertising agencies go to affiliate networks is that they turn to partner marketers who are actively looking for new promotional products.

HOW TO START AN AFFILIATE MARKETING BUSINESS

Before, you start your affiliate marketing business. Here are a few things to keep in mind. You can now become an advertiser or publisher.

There is no right or wrong answer to this, but if you have a product you want to sell. Being an advertiser and being an advertiser is not a bad thing to promote your product.

This is a serious win-win situation and you will not have to pay a commission if you do not trade as a trader in a partner market. If they do, you will make money before you pay.

Or you can become a partner marketer (publisher). Start a blog or start a YouTube channel, connect with your audience, promote your product to your audience, and make money if they buy something.

Note: You do not need to own a product to sell, as most people use the ad reseller (publisher) route. However, this is not as easy as it takes time to generate enough traffic to make money.

Become an advertiser

Do you want to sell your product or are affiliate marketers promoting it? Well, being an advertiser is the right way for you! First, you need a product, and if you don't have one yet, fine.

- **Step 1. Product idea:**
  When coming up with a product idea, it is advisable to look for something already popular. Ask yourself if people want it. Products that are not in demand will not give you money.
  Ask yourself, what motivates you to buy someone?Some people buy a car so they can travel long distances faster.Many people buy a coffee machine, so you can make coffee at home or in the office.Most people buy a gaming computer so they can play these graphics-heavy games more smoothly.Do you remember when fidget spinning manufacturers were very popular? Well, many people have formulated this idea and created different versions of the fidget spinner. I recommend looking for a digital product as there is no risk of such a large investment in the production process as everything is going to make money online. There is no cost to create a digital product.

Here are some resources to learn how to create your digital product.

- E-books
- Online training
- Podcast

- **Step 2. Product creation:**
  If you do not have the knowledge and skills to produce your digital product. You can hire someone to help you by offering them a percentage of your profits.

- **Step 3. To preview, copy, and paste it:**

Once you have created the product, you can start previewing the product. This is the same method that film producers use to predict a movie before it is released.

- **Step 4. Sell your product:**
  You can then join the affiliate network and find partner marketers to promote your product. Or you can create your affiliate program.
  I recommend checking ClickFunnels as they offer one of the best sales funnel generating software so you can manage partner marketers on one platform.

Become a Publisher

- **Step 1. Select a platform:**
  Unlike an advertiser, you don't have to think about creating a real product. Instead, start testing your product on your phone. This can be in the form of a blog post or a YouTube video.
  I also recommend creating an email list using an email marketing provider. That way, you'll always be able to connect instead of hoping your audience will come back and see your content. And how to do a webinar that can be learned, it's a great way to add value and create an email list.

- **Step 2. Summarize the product list and write a product review.**
  Once you've compiled a list of products you want to promote, it's important to know how to write a good product overview. It is important to include the following information.

  - Product name
  - Product creator
  - Product cost
  - Product Review
  - Product advantages and disadvantages
  - Evaluation of conclusion

When choosing a product, consider how relevant it is to your audience. How to help them? If the product you offer is of poor quality. You at least please your audience to avoid wasting money.However, if it is a good product, it will help customers make informed purchasing decisions.No matter what you see, and you need to be faithful to it. Otherwise, it will turn off your audience if they just try to bet faster than them.When reviewing a product, I recommend trying the product first so you can relate to it.

- **Step 3. Add affiliate links**
  In your product overview, you can include affiliate links that direct customers to the actual product if they are interested. This way, the advertiser knows that the customer will contact you.
  Collaborative links will give you a network of advertisers or partners. Here's what my affiliate link looks like in ClickFunnels.Adding affiliate links to product reviews is a good start, but it takes a lot of traffic to make some serious money. As the business is based on repeat customers, you will hear over and over again that "money is on this list".

- **Step 4. Doing Repeated Business Using Email Marketing:**
  Email Marketing: As I mentioned several times during this lesson, email is the best way to market to an existing audience.It all invites you to sign up for a lead in your email brochure.To increase conversions, it is better to direct the subscriber to the confirmation page, not to say thank you for the ordered message.

  You can also use the sidebar to get your reader's email address. This will allow you to see your rejection form no matter what blog you are posting. Here is an example from a close friend of mine.

Remember that your subscribers are registered for a specific reason. Think about why they should order, send an email, or run a campaign. Don't make all these sales when sending the email. Instead, offer them value. For example, you can also post new blog posts or product reviews.

You can also use **YouTube videos** depending on what you are watching. Let's say you're trying to control a new iPhone. If you were a user, would you read about it or see it in reality? Now if you are going to sell a digital product, you can even have a consulting service. You can use a tool like ClickFunnels to open a page where people can register on the webinar.

After setting up the landing page for your upcoming webinar. Just share them you need to pre-register on social media so you can sign up before people post.

Webinars can be organized using services such as WebinarOnAir or Google Hangout (completely free). It's as easy as using FaceTime or a video chat app.We will discuss about the Webinar in the next lesson.

Here are some things you can do as part of your web lesson.

- Introduce yourself so your audience can learn more about you. (Nice to meet you)
- Introduce product features.
- Demonstrate the actual product directly with your own hands.
- Discuss the pros and cons of the product.
- Explain what you think about the product after use.
- Finally, we put our sales in order. Why should your audience buy the product?

Before organizing these webinars, contact the product developer and let them know first. If they give your audience a unique discount code, feel free to ask them.

This is a great way to reach an audience with a bargain that increases conversions.

Finally, use **PPC advertising** to expand your affiliate marketing business. It takes time for a blog or YouTube channel to grow organically. That's why many affiliate marketers look at paid advertising.

From personal experience, Facebook ads are great for video campaigns, and Google ads are targeted to search. Now I don't have to deal with PPC explanations. Instead, here's a great article comparing both Facebook ads and Google ads.

I prefer organic traffic to paid traffic, so what if you stop making paid traffic? Traffic stops.

However, PPC advertising is great if you want people to sign up for your webinar, generate more sales, or build your email list. It is recommended that you do not offer this if you are only going to sell 1 piece.

You need to look at the lifelong value of the customer. If you use PPC ads to get an email address, you can get back in touch via email without spending the extra money to target the same customer through PPC ads.

MODULE 9
WEBINAR MARKETING

WHAT IS A WEBINAR?

The Most New Marketing Strategy for Online Businesses, Webinars are short for web-seminar terms. Webinars allow anyone to create online shows that can be watched live. Webinars are a format of events that take place online and are also attended online. With this format, anyone can create talk shows, seminars, discussions, and workshops with only a camera and internet connection.

Webinars are an effective and fresh marketing strategy. Because you can make the audience feel close to the type of communication that is personal and interactive. But at the same time, you do it with so many people. So, your marketing strategy can cover quality and quantity at the same time.

BENEFITS OF WEBINAR FOR ONLINE BUSINESS MARKETING STRATEGIES

In addition to the right marketing strategies, there are other benefits that you will get through webinars. Some of the benefits of webinars are:

Increase brand awareness of your business.

Webinars can be used as a medium to tell the benefits of your business. Through the same medium, you can provide useful information and tips for customers.

Presenting more value in front of (potential) customers.

Like freebies in the form of ebooks or checklists, webinars are very strategic to be used to educate customers. The more people feel the benefits of the brand, the more they also engage and feel the need

Soliciting suggestions and feedback

Armed with tons of interactive features such as chat, polls, surveys, tests, and integration into Twitter, you can immediately find out what your audience wants.

- **Showing a more expert image than competitors**. Just like blogs on websites, webinars will show how knowledgeable and your capabilities. This is what then makes you look more serious and expert in his field.
- **Gather leads.** Just like email marketing, webinars can be used to collect the names and email addresses of (potential) potential customers. This method makes it easy for you when you want to send promotional info to them.
- **Save time and promotion costs**. Creating offline events is expensive. Many technical things need to be prepared. Already so, not necessarily also more successful offline events. If you have a tight promotional budget, you can use webinars for more efficient promotions.

HOW TO PLAN A WEBINAR?

This is the moment you've been waiting for. In this section, we will discuss how to plan and create a webinar. We deliberately discuss the two separately because there are so many things that need to be discussed.

Planning a Webinar: What Must Be Prepared?

The preparation was never in vain. That is precisely what drives you to success. This is also the case if you want to do promotions via webinars. Don't let your webinar session end up embarrassing. Make sure you run the 10 steps below before running the webinar.

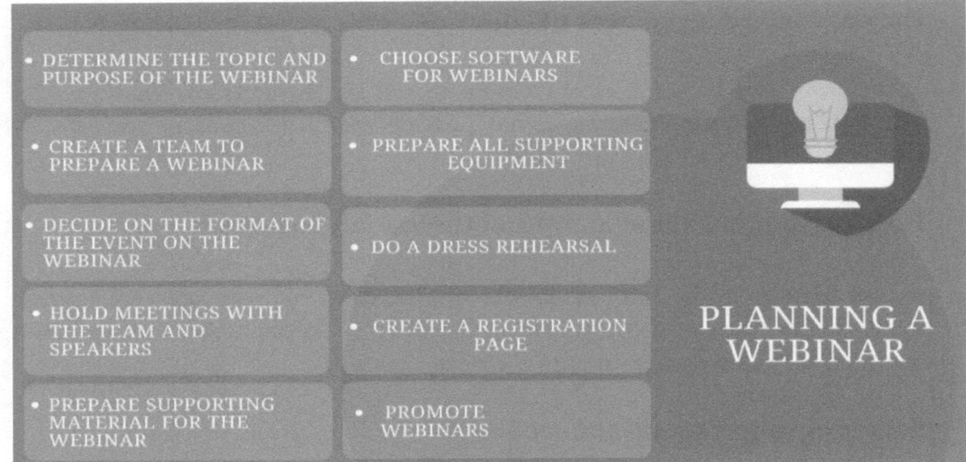

Determine the topic and purpose of the webinar

Before discussing things that are too technical, you need to make sure the topic and purpose of creating a webinar. By determining these two things in advance, you will be helped to design webinar sessions more precisely.

After meeting the topic and purpose of the webinar, continue by answering the next two questions. First, who is your target audience? Then second, how long will the webinar session last?

If necessary, try to research by watching other webinars. As much as possible, look for webinars that have similar topics that you want to raise. That way, you have a benchmark for how you should execute webinars.

Create a team to prepare a webinar

Creating a webinar alone is risky. Therefore, try to create a team for your webinar project. No need a big team, the important thing is some people are divided to do these three things:

- **Coordinator**-The coordinator takes care of things behind the scenes of the webinar project. From planning topics, choosing speakers, designing promotional strategies, opening registration forms, to opening webinar events. Not infrequently, the coordinator also interviews the speaker during the session.

- **The Speaker-** The speaker is the person responsible for the quality of the webinar content. He must master the content and deliver it well. It would be great when the speaker mastered the use of webinar software. Nothing else so that the session can run smoothly.

- **Assistant-** There are three roles at once that can be done by one (or more) assistants. First, the assistant can make sure technical things run smoothly during the webinar. He can tell like an inaudible voice or video is dead. Second, give a provocation of questions in the question and answer session. Third, do research and find answers to make it easier for the speaker to answer questions.

With a clear division of tasks, you are less likely to encounter a blunder during the webinar session.

Decide on the format of the event on the webinar

After detailing the job description, it is time to choose the format of the webinar event. There are four common formats used when creating events:

Single speaker — this format presents just one speaker in a session. This speaker is responsible for guiding the entire event. Include answers & questions from the audience. At first glance, this format is more practical because you don't need to coordinate with many people. However, this format is only able to offer one point of view in the discussion.

A talk show or interview — the format of the event presents one interviewer and one speaker, something that makes webinars more flexible. With this kind of format, the audience can see the various viewpoints and experiences of the speaker. Even so, you need to be smart to coordinate with many parties so that the event runs smoothly.

Panel discussion — this format presents many speakers with the help of one moderator. Many points of view can be explored when you use this format. It's just that, you again need to spend extra energy to coordinate with all parties. Not to mention that you have to make sure the speakers don't dominate the conversation.

Interactive — Interactive webinars often contain group exercises or question and answer sessions. This format will be very effective if followed by a limited number of participants. The quality of the webinar session will also depend greatly on the questions and interactions of the participants during the session.

If you intend to use webinars as a promotional medium, the single speaker format and talk shows are the most commonly used? If you make a webinar as a big celebration event or seminar, then an interactive panel discussion or forum can be an option.

Hold meetings with the team and speakers

After deciding on the format, it's good to hold a large meeting. Especially to discuss matters relating to webinar content.

Discuss with the speaker. What questions should be thrown in webinars? How much time does it take to discuss a topic? Then, of course, when does the speaker deposit modules or slide material?

Believe me; you do not want to receive it tightly with the date the webinar was held. This is done to avoid drama during the webinar. After all, you also need to edit the material and design the slides to make it look more esthetic.

Prepare supporting material for the webinar

The next step is of course preparing webinar material. If the material is prepared by the speaker, all you have to do is edit it a little and give it a touch of decoration. To be easy when designing it, you can use one of the digital marketing tools like Canva.

There are at least four things that should be included in the slides:

- Technical instructions for following the webinar session- This slide will make it easier for first-time audiences to take part in webinars so they don't get confused.
- It contains a CV or short introduction from the speaker- Not only includes the name but the origin of the organization, position, achievements, and a brief portfolio.
- The slides contain the agenda and topics to be discussed in the webinar.
- The main slide contains material that was presented during the session.

Besides slides, it would be great if you also provided additional material. Checklists, modules, worksheets, audio, transcripts, or whatever may be included.

Choose software for webinars

There are so many software choices for hosting webinars. For example, such as Zoom, EverWebinar, Livestream, WebEx, and so forth. Whichever software you choose, make sure that the software answers your needs. Make sure how many participants the software can accommodate, what features are offered, whether the software provides save webinar session options and software prices.

Prepare all supporting equipment

Prepare all the tools that support webinars. Starting from a closed and conducive room, headphones and mic, plug cables, and a stable internet connection.

Do a dress rehearsal

Not only offline events that need a dress rehearsal, webinars too. The dress rehearsal agenda must be made a mandatory agenda before the webinar is done. Because webinars have many technical elements that must be ensured to run smoothly. Better be safe than sorry, right?

For your dress rehearsals to be effective and efficient, make sure you do the following:

Check all supporting equipment. Check whether the equipment is functioning normally. Can headphones and mic be used? Are the plugs long enough? Did the laptop and browser not crash?

Introduce how to use webinar software to the speaker. Make sure the speaker understands very well how to operate the software. This must be done especially when the webinar format taken is a single speaker. At a minimum, teach the speaker how to turn on sounds, display slides, and enable screen capture to simulate something.

Do dress rehearsals like doing a live webinar? Create unlimited webinar sessions specifically for simulations. Perform evaluations related to technical matters and also the content. Is the content order correct? What is the tempo of content delivery? Is the time allocation for the webinar sufficient?

Only through this preparation can you truly reduce the possibility of technical problems when hosting webinars.

Create a registration page

After all the technical and content preparation is ready, continue to create a registration page. If you want it simple, you can create a Google form on WordPress. This method is more practical and saves time.

But if you want more professional and maximum, it never hurts to create a special landing page. On the landing page, you can enter a supporting story in the style of Sorelle Amore that was discussed earlier. To make landing pages easier, you can use the page builder Elementor.

Promote Webinars

The preparation is almost complete. Now, all you have to do is intensify webinar promotions. Several options can be done for this promotion:

Create a blog article related to the topic of the webinar. Blog articles are a great medium to explain topics at length. Here, you can tell us why the topics covered in the webinar are so important. Do not forget to include supporting data and an explanation of why the webinar is useful.

Promote via social media. People spend hours opening social media. So, promotion on social media should not escape from your radar. Make sure all the social media programs you use are used to promote webinars. Invite friends and colleagues to share promotional content. If necessary, install Facebook Ads and Instagram Ads as well.

Promote via newsletter. Newsletters are also one of the right ways to promote webinars. Instead, through this medium, you can reach customers in a personal way. To create a top-notch newsletter, use the Mailchimp platform.

MODULE 10
VIRAL MARKETING

WHAT IS VIRAL MARKETING?

Viral marketing (viral promotion) is a popular advertising campaign technique in which representatives of the target audience themselves are the main distributor of information about the company/service. With this approach, there is no traditional description of the benefits of the product and a call to buy it; there is not always even a direct indication of the product. Such an advertising campaign involves originality and is aimed at resonance. The message should "catch on" to people who saw it, and provoke sharing with your friends on social networks and offline. Viral ads can be video, text, image, hearing, game, program, or e-book.

GOALS FOR VIRAL MARKETING

In the marketing sphere, there is an opinion that a satisfied customer will advise a service or product that they like to two or three acquaintances. He will share negative impressions with about ten people. It is this behavior mechanism that often uses viral marketing on the Internet and beyond.

The goal of the marketer, in this case, is to detect people with high social significance (SNP - Social Networking Potential) and form a viral message that will interest them. The number of people with whom they share information depends on how much they will be interested.

VIRAL PROMOTIONS METHOD

Pass along

People independently send advertising messages to each other: videos, pictures, etc., because they attract attention and like. An example would be the popular PSY video - "Gangnam Style", which was the first on YouTube to break the 1 billion page share.

Incentivised Viral (Incentive)

Promises users a bonus for certain actions. The goal, in this case, is not just the promotion of a product or service, but the creation of a platform for long-term and fruitful relations with the target audience. For example, the "Mediamarkt" campaign, when visitors were offered to take "Take it away in 50 seconds". Clients filled out a short questionnaire and started a "race" in the departments of a household appliance store, taking with them everything that fit into their hands. This was given 50 seconds. The most common example from social networks is viruses like "Become a subscriber to our community, repost this message to your wall and take part in the drawing of your smartphone/car/perfume".

Undercover (Secretive Method)

This is one of the most effective options for viral promotion of a product/service. It is based on the uniqueness and originality of the content. In this case, they do not open the advertising message and intrigue around it. For example, when Google launched its social network, Google+ issued personalized invitations to register. Otherwise, it was impossible to get into it.

Buzz (Rumors)

This is a risky method that is not always correct, and in some cases can harm the brand. The goal is to attract the attention of the audience in any way.

RULES FOR SUCCESSFUL VIRAL MARKETING

Ease of distribution

It is necessary to create conditions when it is easy for a person to view the content himself and simply transfer it further. For example, you do not need to register to watch the video by reference. You open the page and get the content.

Uniqueness

It must be remembered that the virus will work only once. Then a stable immunity will develop to it. Without changes and new ideas, such advertising does not work.

High-speed spread

The advertising message should not stop. Marketers have calculated that the virus has only three days to spread. If during this time at least 30% of the target audience does not become recognizable, there is almost no chance of success. To increase the speed often attract influential media people who will affect the target audience.

Competent optimization

Without hashtags, "Share" buttons on social networks, links, and other "hooks", a virus campaign is worthless. So you can simplify the distribution of content, make it more accessible.

Resources for posting

After creating a viral video or message, it must be successfully launched in the target audience. This process is called "viral culture." The choice of sites depends on the characteristics of Central Asia - its age, interests, nature of behavior on the Internet. As a resource for sowing use:

- Social network
- Blogs (Well Visited)
- Information Portals
- Communities and Forums
- Video hosting (e.g. YouTube)

BENEFITS OF VIRAL MARKETING

Economic benefit

Advertising on TV, in addition to the budget for creating a video, will require serious investment in a rental on as many channels as possible. Viral marketing is the distribution of the information you need for free. People themselves share the video/message, happy to discuss the details.

Formation of a loyal audience.

The user receives a link to original and interesting content from trusted, in his opinion, sources. Usually, these are friends, large information, or entertainment resources, well-known bloggers, etc. Such distribution does not require your activity, it looks natural and causes interest.

No restrictions on censorship and the Advertising Act.

This is one of the important incentives for the development and popularity of viral marketing. Often, the public interest is turned to forbidden topics: sexuality and scandals. On television, there will be problems using them. Also, under the Law on Advertising on TV, alcohol and tobacco products cannot be promoted. Many goods and services, the dissemination of information about which is traditionally difficult, have found their place in the global network if the distribution is implicit.

Long life cycle and unlimited time.

Commercials on TV are shown only at a time strictly determined by marketers when the target audience is supposedly on the screen. On the Internet, information is in constant motion and does not stop. People transmit links to a video or an advertising post to each other, viewing content at a convenient time and an unlimited number of times. Experts say that viral advertising can exist for two to three years and remain recognizable.

DISADVANTAGES OF VIRAL MARKETING

Need to use other advertising activities.

Despite the many benefits of viral marketing, you cannot use it alone. To fully reveal all the possibilities of such advertising can only be combined with other types of advertising activity. However, it is worth remembering that even the most successful campaign will not help when products and services do not meet the expectations of customers and customers.

Need for the ongoing support of interest.

The fire of hype that erupted around the viral campaign needs to be constantly maintained. Without additional sources of information or new portions of content, within two weeks, interest in the brand/product/service will drop significantly.

The "virus" cannot be affected.

When launching a viral campaign, you should be prepared for the end of your participation in her life. Attempts to influence the development of events or to correct the direction will be futile or lead to negative consequences. Therefore, it is very important to carefully prepare and think through the advertising campaign in advance to the smallest detail.

Dependence on luck.

The mood of the target audience is not always possible to predict. Sometimes even the best-planned viral campaigns do not have the expected effect. Therefore, you should not use only this type of marketing when promoting a product.

EXAMPLES OF VIRAL MARKETING

WWE (World Wrestling Entertainment)

In 2007, this organization touted the return of the famous wrestler Chris Jericho. To do this, she launched a series of 15-second videos on various sites. They contained encrypted messages and references to quotes from the Bible. The intrigue was that in English Jericho is the name of the biblical city of Jericho. Most often in the commercials, you could see the text "Save us" and "The Second Coming".

Old Spice

A good example of an active and effective viral ad campaign. Old Spice creates catchy and funny videos. All of them are united by a common theme of male excellence. The idea itself is very extensive. The company conducts offline events on its basis, creates promotional sites, and leads communities on social networks. At some point, a regular ad campaign turned into a viral one. Internet users began to shoot remakes and skits, create ironic images, etc. This raised the ratings of Old Spice products significantly higher than expected.

MODULE 11
INFLUENCER MARKETING

Influencer marketing has recently become a fairly common phrase on the sunny side of the Alps. Companies and agencies that have found that social media marketing no longer works the way it did years ago have found a new way to bring people closer to their content, products, services - with the help of influencers who are already recognizable and people trust.

People trust their friends and colleagues the most at the buying decision stage. More so than advertisements and "fake testimonials," this is still a mandatory part of any sales site. As if people still read fictional stories and believe everything that marketers write on a website. Ratings of products or services are much better on appropriate platforms, but here we are still well behind the times.

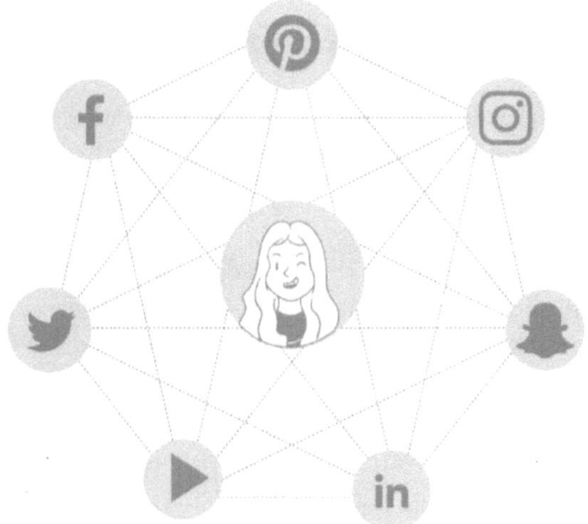

WHAT IS INFLUENCER MARKETING?

"Influencers" who cover certain topics (bloggers, athletes, celebrities, etc.) and are genuine in doing so tend to have quite a few followers, readers, and fans. People identify with them much more than they do with the people in the ads, or with the "stock photos" posted on the site. Influencers have their channels through which they communicate, and if marketers know how to recognize them correctly and allow them to be creative themselves, such campaigns can be much more successful than endless likes on Facebook.

Influencer marketing is creating content through its influencers - for brands, for services, for products. This content can be various tests, brand mentions, photos, or any other material that influencers post on their social networks or their media.

EARN IN PAID INFLENCER MARKETING

There are two ways. In Slovenia, everyone would like to use the first method, but in the world, the second method is much more used. Earned means you have a good relationship with the brand. That you don't get direct payment for your posts (you could also say that you are the "ambassador" of the brand you help with your posts). On the other hand, there are paid influencer marketing, where you get paid for what you do for the brand - the price of course depends on the "reaction" and especially on the niche market. Visibility is also important.

IMPORTANT BUILDING BLOCKS OF INFLUENCER MARKETING

There are three important building blocks in the world with which companies that manage influencers also operate and, based on that, determine the amounts they allocate to influencers:

- Reach/influencers have their channels through which they can reach a large number of consumers. These can be their social media channels, blogs, or anything else where they are recognized.

- Original content/influencers create content that is authoritative and, above all, effective for brands

- Consumer trust / because influencers have behind them users they trust, then we are at the beginning of this record - people trust friends and acquaintances

EXAMPLES OF INFLUENCER MARKETING

Recently, there are more and more wishes and expectations in this area in Slovenia as well. The companies found that they threw a lot of money into advertising on Facebook and that what they expected didn't happen. They are now discovering influencer marketing and each campaign still has a portion of the money set aside for it. What does it look like abroad and at home?

- Kim Kardashian posts a photo of the "product" on Instagram - she's paid handsomely for it, as her reach is enormous. With us, a fashion blogger gets a product and then the company expects a couple of posts of this product on its social networks - without payment of course.

HOW TO REACH?

The word is not a horse! If you have someone at the "point" who could help you with promotion or reach new potential customers, then take the time to research something about this person - what he likes to do, how he eats, what his opinion is about your company (if she happened to mention it somewhere). Above all, try to have an open relationship with such a person - a partnership. Much better than if you only have a business relationship with her. Listen to her because she knows more about her followers and readers than you think and can give you a bunch of quality information you don't know. Above all, be honest with her.

Influencer marketing is something that is increasingly appearing in Slovenia as well. Some companies have been presenting this to their clients for a long time, but things are going rather slowly here. And if in the beginning influencers were rewarded with products, now that is changing as well. Of course, the amounts depend a lot on the reach, the authenticity, and most of all, the ability to create different brand-related content.

MODULE 12
DOMAIN AND HOSTING

WHAT IS DOMAIN AND HOSTING?

In this lesson, we will look at what is domain and hosting. You will certainly come across these two concepts if you want to have your website. To understand what a domain and hosting is and to make the right choice for you, I recommend you to read the following information. With this lesson, I want to tell you what a domain and hosting is and help you in choosing a site.

How exactly they work and how they connect. I also told you that to have a site, you have all files that build the site and you want to share them. Let's imagine that john decides to quit his job and start his own business in the field of tourist services. To be able to offer services, he wants to make a website. But since he has no set-aside budget, he decides to learn on his own. So John creates the site, ie he creates the files and now he has to share them via a URL so that everyone can see them.

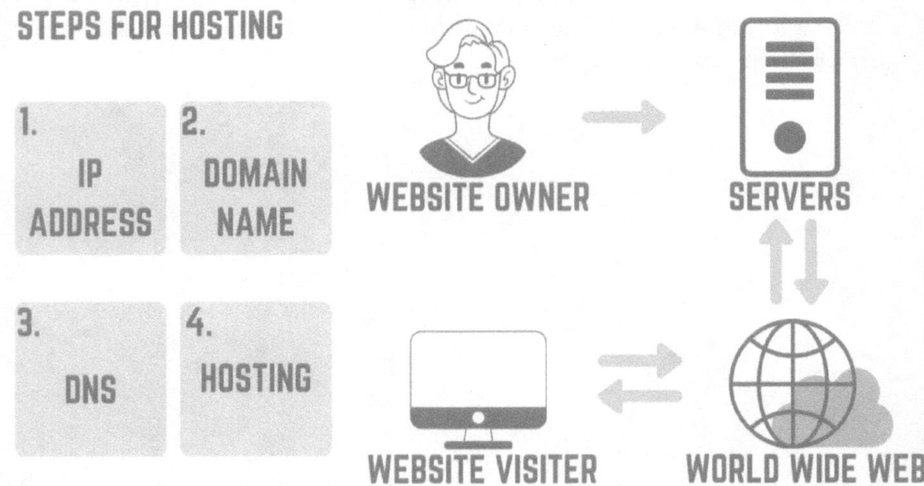

But, how? Every computer or device connected in the local network has its name called "MAC address". Both on the local network and the global network, i.e on the Internet, each computer has another name called an IP address. That means each computer has two names. It's like all your relatives call you Rahul, but when you go out in public they call you Sameer. Both names are yours and you use them. So computers have two names. One for the internal networks and one for the external one.

WHAT IS AN IP ADDRESS?

Every computer that has access to the global network has a name called an IP address. IP address represents something like: 172.217.7.238. This is the IP address of google and if you type this in your browser, google will open.

So, back to John. He created the site and knows his IP address. He sends it to Partima, who wants to visit the most popular tourist destination at the moment.Namely Dubai, with great enthusiasm and desire, Pratima opens the site waiting to see the offer for the desired destination. But surprisingly for her, the site does not open. "There's no website at all," she exclaims. "Can you imagine what a disappointment that is for a young lady?" Who wants to learn so much about the foreign culture of the Middle East?This is because John's computer is locked for external access. That is, John's computer has access to the Internet, but other computers do not have access to John's computer, because we would not have personal computers? And all our files would be shared. But on the other hand, John can't show his site. Therefore, it needs a special program to serve as a filtering mechanism. It allows computers only to the files on the site. But not to all the personal files on his computer. This program is called a server.

WHAT IS SERVER?

That is when another computer requests to access John's computer through its IP address, the server grants access. That is, it only serves the files that John wants to share. This explanation of a server is very simple to understand. In general, the server does a lot more things that I don't need to burden you with informatively at the moment. Nowadays, very few people use their home computers for servers. Because, it requires daily maintenance, high knowledge of technology, and experience in this field. If you've heard of the profession of a system administrator, this is a person who maintains the servers of a company or firm. In general, server computers are quite different from home computers. They are designed to respond instantly to multiple requests. That is, they must be very fast and extremely precise.

Maintaining a server involves time and expense because the server computer is connected 24 hours a day to the network. And if a problem arises, it must be fixed quickly. If you are interested in youtube there are a lot of videos on this topic - how to make a server from your home computer. But I strongly recommend that you contact a company that offers this service. Because the costs will certainly not be higher and thus you will save time. The people working in the company will always take care of the maintenance of the server if you have any problems.

WHAT IS DOMAIN AND HOSTING COMPANY?

Such companies that offer servers are called hosting companies. These are the companies that have large and powerful computers that store the files for our sites. Quite simply, in the following lines, it will become even clearer what a domain and hosting are.

So John decides to turn to a large company that offers to host... Decides to find out what is a domain and hosting. Register and pay the required amount for the service. They give him a place on the server where he can put his files. Everything is great. John has a place but he remembers that he doesn't have a name... i.e he has to connect with this place in some way... And since John is already in class with these things, he calls and tells them that he wants an IP address. The operator tells him - If you have no problems on foot, we will give you an IP address... but don't you think it will be a little difficult for people to remember this IP address to enter your site?

WHAT IS DOMAIN AND URL?

Precisely because IP addresses are difficult to remember and mean nothing, it has been decided that they are associated with some text that means something... This is the URL of your site... this URL is called a domain. That is, the name of your site and the URL address that appears in the browser field is your domain. And when Pratima wants to enter John's website, she writes the domain in the browser. Her computer sends a request to the server that it wants to open the files on this domain, and the server returns a response. And if there are files to this domain, the site serves them and displays them. Pratima is happy and looking forward to the date for her dream trip.

All the names, events, and destinations in this lesson are completely random. This was the tutorial for today I hope you found it useful and you understood what domain and hosting are. In the next lesson, I will tell you about 4 important steps to follow when building a plan for your site. With these tutorials, I want to help you understand the sites and the process of creating them so you can make the right choice for you. Thank you for your attention, if you want to learn more useful tutorials, you can subscribe to my youtube channel via the subscribe button.

DIFFERENT TYPES OF WEB HOSTING

There are four different types of hosting servers: shared, virtual private server (VPS), dedicated, and cloud hosting.

While all types of servers will act as the storage center of your website, they differ in the amount of storage capacity, control, technical knowledge requirements, server speed, and reliability.

- Shared Hosting
- **Virtual Private Server (VPS) Hosting**
- **Dedicated Server Hosting**
- **Cloud Hosting**

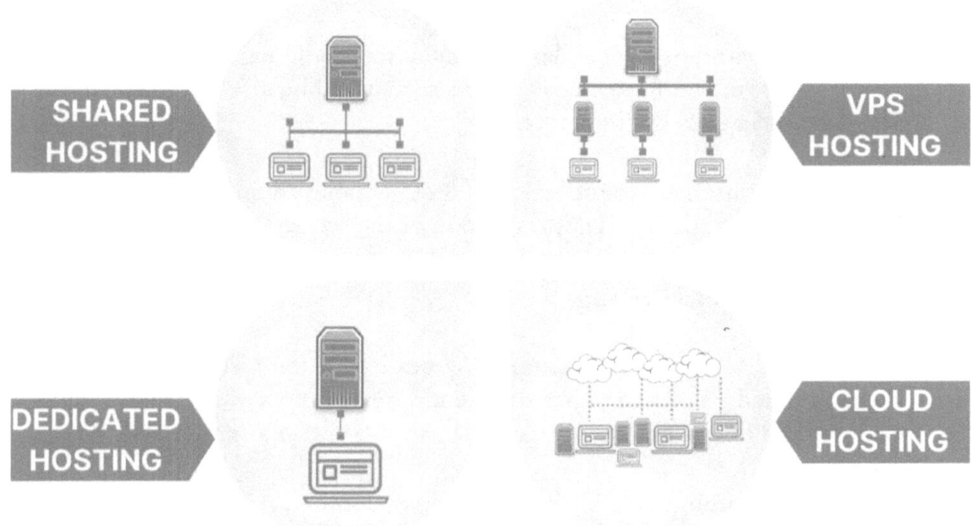

Shared Hosting

In shared hosting, the website is hosted on the same server as many other sites, ranging from a few to hundreds or thousands. Typically, all domains can share a common set of server resources, such as RAM and CPU.

Because the cost is extremely low, most moderately trafficked websites running standard software are hosted on this type of server. Shared hosting is also widely accepted as a hosting option as it requires minimal technical knowledge.

- **Disadvantages** - Without root access, limited ability to handle high levels of traffic, or spikes, site performance may be affected by other sites on the same server.

- **How much to spend** - No more than $ 10 when registering.

Virtual Private Server (VPS) Hosting

A virtual private hosting server divides the server into virtual servers, where each website is hosted on its dedicated server, but they share a server with several different other users.

Users can have root access to their own virtual space and a better secure hosting environment with this type of hosting. Websites that need more server-level control but do not want to invest in a dedicated server.

- **Disadvantages** - The limited ability to handle high levels of traffic or spikes, the performance of your site may still be affected to some extent by other sites on the server.

- **How much to spend -** $ 20 - $ 60 / mole; additional costs for those who need additional customization of the server or special software.

Dedicated Server Hosting

A dedicated server offers maximum control over the webserver where your website is stored - You can only rent an entire server. Your website (s) is the only website stored on the server.

- **Disadvantages -** With great force comes ... well, a higher price. Dedicated servers are very expensive and are only recommended for those who need maximum control and better server performance.

- **How much to spend -** $ 80 / m and above; price based on server specifications and additional services.

Cloud Hosting

Cloud hosting offers an unlimited opportunity to handle high traffic or traffic spikes. Here's how it works: A team of servers (called a cloud) works together to host a group of websites. This allows multiple computers to work together to handle high levels of traffic or spikes for any particular website.

- **Disadvantages** - Many cloud hosting settings do not offer root access (needed to change server settings and install some software products) at a higher cost.

- **How much to spend** - $ 30 and above; Cloud hosting users are usually charged based on usage.

MODULE 13
WORDPRESS

WHY CHOOSE A WORDPRESS WEBSITE?

Not confident with website content management systems (CMS) or not sure why choose WordPress? Then this lesson is just for you - you will find out what it is and why you should install WordPress.

WHAT IS WEBSITE CONTENT MANAGEMENT SYSTEM (CMS)?

CMS is software that allows you to change the content of a website without any programming or other complex technical knowledge. Imagine you have a website that describes the services or products you offer. If you want to change the description or add a new product, the high-quality CMS allows you to make these changes very simply - with just a few button presses.

No need to worry about technical details as the new content will look like posting product photos or other related information - everything is controlled in a simple control panel. If you deal with Microsoft Word or similar text editors, you should have no problems with well-made CMS.

CMS can easily implement new features (this is done with the help of plugins). It's also usually easy to change design templates - you can change the design of your website in minutes.

WHY WORDPRESS?

Often inexperienced Internet users mix two different platforms - a free blogging platform (WordPress.com) and a complete content management system (WordPress.org). Although both were used as platforms for blogs more than 10 years ago, WordPress CMS (WordPress CMS) has come a long way since then - with the help of this system, it is possible to create practically any website - online store, representative company website, portfolio, forum, ad portal, etc. Due to its unparalleled capabilities, more than a quarter of websites worldwide use WordPress CMS. It is also used by world-class companies such as eBay, Facebook, Google, LinkedIn, Sony, Disney, The New York Times, Discovery, and many more.

WHAT KIND OF WEBSITE CAN BE CREATED WITH WORDPRESS

WordPress CMS is suitable for different types of websites:

- For blogs
- Business representative sites
- Online stores
- Ad portals
- Business directories
- Sites for the presentation of works (portfolio)
- Forums
- Informational / wiki type sites
- Photography sites
- Websites of schools or other educational institutions
- Closed blogs or information systems that can only be viewed by logged-in users

CREATE A WORDPRESS WEBSITE IN EASY 3 STEPS

There are two things you need to do before creating a WordPress site:
- The idea for a domain name (this will be the name of your site, for eg. Partimakitchen.com).
- Web hosting account (this is where pieces of your website are stored on the Internet).

Step 1. Purchase a Domain and Hosting

The biggest mistake that beginners make when building a site or blog is choosing the wrong blogging platform. For 95% of users, it makes more sense to use WordPress.org, also known as self-hosted WordPress. Why? Since it is free to use, you can install plugins, customize the design of your online commerce site, and most importantly - make money from your site without restrictions.

You've probably heard that WordPress is free. You may be wondering why? What's the catch? There is no trick. It's free because you have to set up and manage the site yourself.

In other words, you need a domain name and web hosting.WordPress is free but domain and hosting will be paid according to your preference. Having your domain will make your site look much more professional and beautiful than if your site is part of another domain. Dedicated Having your hosting means that your site will load quickly and will always be online, which is very important.

Now you have to sign up on any web hosting provider site, like hostinger.com, bluehost.com, godaddy.com.

Let's assume you've decided to start with a shared hosting plan on bluehost.com. Here are your options:

Now, Select a plan and link your domain with your hosting, If you are not buying your domain name yet, then you can create a new domain here, then click on 'next'.

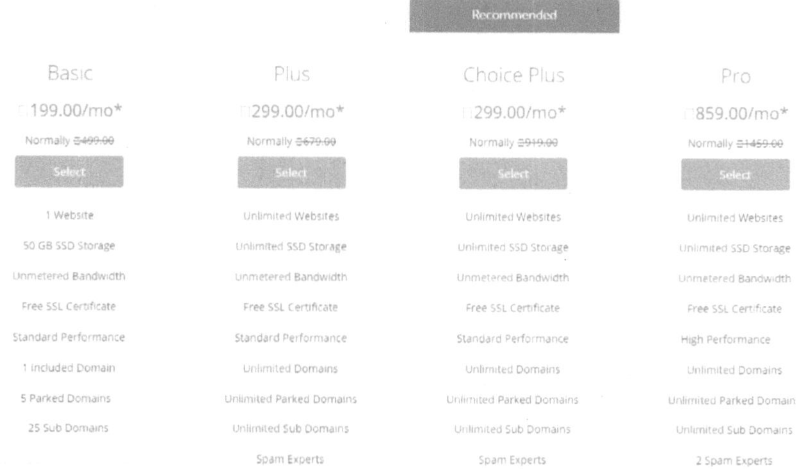

Confirm the purchase and complete the registration process, Buy your domain and hosting. I recommend bluehosting.com, but of course, you can choose other hosting companies as long as they are reliable and easy. When you are ready, go to the next step and you will soon find out how we will make the site.

Use Google Single Sign-On to make creating your account even easier.

G   Sign in with Google

Account Information

All fields are required unless otherwise noted.

First Name

Last Name

(optional) Business Name

Country   India

Street Address

City

State/Province   Please select a state

Pincode

Phone Number   +91.   (123) 456-7890   Ext

Select another country code

*Email Address

STEP 2: Install WordPress and WordPress theme (template).

Once you purchase your domain and hosting you are only a little further away from creating your website. For me, this has always been the most enjoyable part of the whole process.

It's time to drive your site. The most important part of how to make a website is the installation of the platform. The first thing we need to do is install WordPress on your domain.

WordPress installation

There are 2 main ways to install WordPress - one extremely easy and the other a little more difficult. I suggest we choose the easier one!

To create a site with WordPress use the one-click installation option.

Massively all reliable hosting companies offer the option to install WordPress with just 1 click of the mouse.

If you have registered with bluehost.com or any other company you will find this option in your control panel (or cPanel)

Here's what you need to do:

- Log in with your account.
- Click on Hosting Accounts
- Click Login to cPanel
- At the bottom, find where it says Softaculous Apps Installer and click on WordPress

- Click Install Now. Select the domain where you want to install WordPress and fill in the settings.

Or you can do it manually (if necessary).

If for some strange reason (for example if the hosting company does not offer this option) you do not have the option to automatically install WordPress then look here:

It's time to choose a theme for your site.

Once we have completed the installation of WordPress on your domain will load a very simple theme. This is one of the standard themes that come with WordPress.But I guess you don't want to be like everyone else. That's why you need to choose a theme that best suits your vision of what the site should look like. This is the most pleasant part. There are thousands of great themes that are professionally crafted and created from which you can choose and customize your website.

Here's how to find a better theme for your site.

Log in to the WordPress Dashboard. If you are not sure how it works just type https: //mysite.com/wp-admin (replace 'my site' with your domain name)
Here's what a WordPress Dashboard looks like:
Even if it seems confusing to you, don't worry, you will soon notice that everything is designed and arranged extremely well and efficiently. Here's what you need to do:

Free themes

Look on the left where it says Appearance, place the mouse there, and then click on Themes.
This will take you to the topics you have currently installed. Click Add New. Here you have access to over 1500 free themes and every day you can discover a new one

Paid topics

Free is free but if you want something professional or more elegant than the themes you can find here I recommend you head to themeforest.net (affiliate link) where you can find one of the largest compilations of themes on different topics and different prices.

As you can see, installing a new theme is extremely easy. You can use different words or filters to search for a topic that will suit your taste. Finding the perfect theme can take time. But I love this process because this is the time when you see your site come to life. So it's worth the time. It is good to look for topics that are said to be responsive. This means that they will look good even on mobile devices such as phones and tablets. You can use this word as a filter to make sure you choose the right topic.

Install your new theme

Once you've chosen a theme, just click Install and then Activate. It is. Important: Switching between different topics will not delete your posts and pages or text. You can change the themes you use as often as you want, everything you have written or uploaded will be where it was.

STEP 3: Site settings, Pages, menu, and layout.

How do I add content and how do I create new pages?

Once you've installed your chosen theme, it's time to think about creating the content. Let's take a look at the basics that are good to know:

Add and edit pages and posts

If you want to add new pages like Blog, About, Contact me, etc.
- Look in the menu on the left and look for where it says Pages and click Add New
- Clicking there will take you to something very similar to MS Word. Add a title, text, pictures, and other things you want and click Save as Draft to save the plain text, and when you are ready to publish it click Publish.

Add pages to the menu

If you want your new page to be visible on the menu
- In the box on the left, click Appearance -> Menus
- Find the page you just made and add it by clicking the box
- And then click Add to Menu

Add and edit posts and articles in WordPress

If you want to have a blog then the field of posts is to which you will pay your attention. You can use different categories to group different posts.

If you want to make a blog to your site you can use categories and posts. For example, if you want to have a category with the name of the blog - you just need to add it to the menu and start writing your posts.

Here's what you need to do:
- Create a new category by going to Posts -> Add New
- Once you have finished writing your post you need to add it to the category you want.
- Once you've created your category, just add it to the menu and you're done.

Personalization and settings

Here I will touch on some of the most commonly asked questions that I have noticed that people have.

Change of Title and Brief Description

The title of your site shows people what your site is. They are also important for the good ranking of your site. In other words, you want to have some of the words you want to qualify for - but spelled normally the way people would put it. It's good to use different titles for different pages. For example, the title of my site is "How to make a site" (If you can't find it, just hover your mouse over the open tab in your browser.) Short description - it is added after the title of each page. My tagline is "how to make a website".

If you want to change them go to Settings-> General and fill in the fields.

Disable the option for comments below posts and pages

Some sites (especially businesses and organizations) do not want visitors to their site to be able to leave comments below their pages.

Here's how to turn this option off:

- While writing a new page, click Skin Options in the upper right corner
- Click on the Discussion box and you will see a allow comments box that will appear below.
- Uncheck allow comments.

If you want to turn off comments on all sides by default

1 go to Settings - Discussion and uncheck all people then post comments on new items

How to put a static main page

If you don't want your homepage to look like a blog, you can change that by making your homepage static. A static page is one that does not change. Unlike a blog where when a new post is published, it will be displayed on the main page. Static will display the same content. To set up a static page

Go to Settings – Reading

Select the static page you want to load on your main page. Home page - is the page that will load on the home page. A post page is what the post categories will look like.

If you do not select a static page, WordPress will display your recent posts on the main page.

Sidebar adjustment

Most WordPress themes have a sidebar on the right (sometimes on the left, in some cases even on both sides)

If you want to get rid of the sidebar or change the things that are displayed there, here's how to do it.
- Go to Appearance - Widgets
- From here you can move and accordingly remove or put the different items you want to display.

There are various boxes that you can even use an HTML box in which you can put HTML code. Widgets are a good way to customize your first site even more. For starters - don't worry about it - for now, just add or remove the things you don't like. Usually, Categories, Meta, and Archives are not needed at all.

Install Extensions (plugins) for additional WordPress functionality

What is an extension?

Extensions or plugins are designed to add additional features and capabilities to WordPress.
Keep in mind that there are over 25,000 free extensions so there are plenty to choose from.

They are easy to install - Click on Extensions - Add more.

Select the extensions you want to install and activate.

To save you time, I have made a list of the most popular plugins that most people use:

- **Contact Form 7** - On my page where you can contact me I have just such a contact form. This is a great feature because it makes it very easy for people to contact you and send you a message. Without having to log in to their emails. If you want to have something like this use this plugin. Here you will find step by step how to set up contact form 7 for your site

- **Yoast SEO** - If you want to optimize your site a little more this plugin is almost a must. It's free and worth it. It allows you to edit and customize your titles, meta descriptions, and more. As such, you can do it on the page itself without having to scroll up and down the WordPress menus.

- **Google Analytics** - If you want to track your traffic just install this plugin and link it to your GA account.

Of course, this is just the tip of the iceberg, Congratulations, this is for now!

You have reached the end of the "how to make a website" guide. If you have followed the steps so far, you should already have a working WordPress site ready. Was it difficult? Last but not least, keep improving your site.

MODULE 14
CREATE A BLOG

WHAT IS BLOG?

A blog is an online resource with regularly updated content (text, images, multimedia). The user who publishes this content is called a blogger. In it, the user shares his thoughts, talks about his life, publishes news, or just informational material. The type and nature of published content are determined by the blogger himself.

WHO NEED A BLOG?

Blogs gained great popularity with the development of Internet technologies when each person had free access to the Internet. Today it is not just an opportunity to share your thoughts with other people, it is an opportunity to earn on your favorite business and gain great popularity.

In the blogosphere, there are frequent cases when a young guy or girl becomes millionaires. Monetization of blogs can bring a decent income. And all that is needed is to regularly publish interesting content. Having a large number of subscribers (readers, viewers), the blogger becomes the object of the attention of advertisers. His audience is loyal and trusts him, therefore, it is well converted.

Subscribers who trust their idol will watch the ad and say "thank you!". Today, advertising with bloggers (hidden, open) is a separate area of Internet marketing. In terms of effectiveness, this promotion method is not inferior to context, SEO, and SMM, which in turn are considered the best ways to promote on the Web.

Therefore, the answer to the question: "who needs blogs?" simple - to everyone. Anyone who wants to earn money, become popular, or just share their thoughts with others.

10 PROFESSIONAL TIPS ON HOW TO CREATE A BLOG

You love to write, you want to say what you think and feel, or you just want to allow people to read interesting content. To date, blogs are perhaps the most popular way to spread information and news. Today, there are thousands of blogs on the Internet and thousands more will be created. However, this should not kill your dream of becoming a popular blogger or having a corporate blog.

Starting a blog is not always as easy as it seems. Even with such an abundance of information that can be found on the Internet and many recommendations from other people, you will still face difficulties, especially if you want the blog to be successful.

The model of blogging is not always the main problem: its development is much more important. Here are some important professional tips to help beginners develop a blog.

Choose the right blog platform.

The main task that novice bloggers face when designing their first blog is choosing the right blogging platform. The good thing is that there are so many good free platforms from which you can choose something that will suit you. Each of them can offer something unusual for your blog, which will help it stand out from the others. This way you can choose a platform depending on your desires and goals. All you need for an easy start is these are a few themes to help you customize your blog.

Choose a specific niche

Niche - this is the topic you will write about in your blog. It needs to be specific to engage and keep readers interested, wanting to come back again. Blog posts must not be too general, as this can confuse readers, and confusion is one of the common reasons bloggers lose their followers. The more specific and specific your content, blog articles are, the more likely you are to attract new users and success to your blog. Consider integrating the blog with an existing site or as a category to it

This is all that is needed to promote the content. If you start maintaining a blog on the site, it will bring significant benefits to you and your work, as well as the ranking of the site itself. This way, readers will be able to easily get to the site at any time and get a clearer idea of your business or products. This is how you do SEO naturally - you attract users with interesting content. You can also add links to your blog to direct your readers to the main site or online store for more information or purchase.

Give readers what they want

Your readers are the key to your success, so you need to give them what they want. Bloggers who offer real value to their readers are the ones who develop successful blogs. Value reflected in the form of useful content. If your readers don't find the content interesting and useful, they won't read it and your blog will never be successful.

When starting a blog, remember that you are not doing it for yourself, but for your readers, and you should publish articles that are interesting to them, not just you.

Choose titles wisely

Try to choose titles with the clearest meaning to grab the readers' attention in a short time. It's also a good idea to use words that are easy to find on the Internet when users start searching for your topic online. Attractive and original titles will not disappoint you when it comes to attracting and retaining readers. Users will like your creativity and will always look forward to the next article. Getting readers' attention online is easy when you arouse their curiosity; give them an emotional text or useful advice.

Blog about what you love

Although we talked a little above that you should write about readers, but you should not forget about yourself. Readers will not like the topics if you do not love the texts in the blog, and this is unlikely to be useful content for the site. The passion you put or not into your texts as a blogger is also felt by readers, so don't risk writing and publishing articles that you don't like. Choose topics that are easy, enjoyable, and about which you can write a lot. This will allow you to write and maintain the blog for a long time.

Use images

Many people love photos, pictures, images. If you look at some of the most successful blogs on the Internet, you will notice the widespread use of images. They add visual interest, so it's important to "dilute" the text with photos and provide the blog with good quality images. It is good to provide readers with a variety (text, photos, graphics) that they will be able to enjoy while browsing the blog. Then everything you write about, including photos and the blog in general, will attract many readers.

Follow the analysis

It is important to know how people get on the blog and how they find you. This way you will know how to improve your blog to attract more readers, as well as what needs to be done to make it easier for your target audience to access. For example, if you have experience with marketing, the analysis will help you analyze the success of your blog. This will pay off all your investment and effort, allowing you to know if it's worth it or not.

Leave room for interaction

People will feel part of the blog if they can interact freely. Therefore, for a blog to be successful, you need to leave some room for interaction with your readers. Encourage readers to give their opinion and leave comments, ask questions they encounter on the topic you are writing about. You also need to respond and help in time for readers to appreciate your attitude towards them. Try to create a community on your blog and be kind to your readers to help them feel part of your blog.

Don't clutter the blog

Sometimes you are so excited at first that you don't realize how you add too much to the blog, which creates chaos and repulses many readers. If you want readers to come back again and again, you need to keep your blog clean, fresh, and easy to navigate. Don't add too many options and features that no one is using or materials that are no longer up to date. Developing a blog should not be a difficult and burdensome task for you. Follow the basic professional tips, write and publish willingly, and then the blog will surely succeed.

Promote Your Blog

After following these steps, I hope you already have created a blog with several articles. It's time to promote it. Basically, after 20-40 articles you will have enough visits from search engines, but you should always promote your blog. Here's how to do it:

- **Paid advertising.** The source of the most visits when you advertise properly. I recommend using Google AdWords, as banners are an outdated form of advertising. Make sure the ad explains the name, content, and purpose of your blog.

- **Guest Blogging.** Select a blog on your topic and write an article about it, provided that there is information about you and your blog in the article. Try it soon - contact a blogger and offer him a guest article on a predetermined topic.

- **Personal Promotion.** Register in a forum on your topic. Share some useful opinions and topics by putting a link/banner to your site in your signature. Believe me, there will be visitors. You will also create a very useful authority for you and your blog by sharing valuable information with others. Another method of personal promotion is commenting on other blogs. Share something valuable like comment and put a link to your blog.

The main sources of traffic on blogs generally come from social bookmarking sites, search engines (mainly Google), and partnerships with other blogs. Why aren't you?

HOW TO MAKE MONEY FROM A BLOG?

We come to the last point of the article - monetizing a blog. It is important not to create a blog just for the money. So I shared that your blog what you are interested in. Making money from a blog is an extra rather than a goal.

Monetize your blog at least a month or two after its public presentation. Then you will have enough visitors and the authority to make money. When visitors see a brand new blog with two or three articles and ads, the goal is clear - just the money.

Four ways to make money from your blog:

- **Pay Per Click**. For all blogs, I recommend Google AdSense. The program pays the most compared to competitors and is extremely easy to use and integrate.

- **Text Link Ads.** A good source of income for most bloggers. You sell links on your site to advertisers. As with Google AdSense, payment is by check. Put a good enough title and explanation in English for advertisers to find and pay you.

- **Pay Per Post.** To use Pay per Post, you must have a blog of at least three months in English. The principle is simple - advertisers pay you to promote their products/sites on your blog through a post. The minimum amount per review is $ 5, and you can rise over $ 100 per paid article.

- **Advertisers.** Contact companies that offer services similar to the topic of your blog. Offer them a specific type of advertising at a reasonable price and expect a response. I wish you luck.

I hope this Lesson has benefited both new and current bloggers.

MODULE 15
E-COMMERCE

WHAT IS E-COMMERCE?

E-Commerce refers to the purchase and sale of services or goods using the Internet and the transfer of money and information to carry out these transactions. E-commerce is often used to refer to the online sale of physical products, but any e-commerce transaction that is facilitated via the Internet can also be added to e-commerce.

While e-commerce refers to all aspects of an online business, e-commerce is specifically concerned with the transaction of goods and services.

CREATE A SUCCESSFUL E-COMMERCE BUSINESS

Creating a successful e-commerce business is much more difficult than building an e-shop. Creating a store is a very simple process, find something to sell, buy a website (or just create an eBay account), draw a logo, and so on –

maybe you already have an e-commerce portal. But you don't have an e-commerce business.

In this lesson, I'll give you tips on how to make your e-commerce business, not just e-commerce. In my opinion, these tips are certainly not limited, but it will be very. Welcome if you take advantage of them:

Understand the structure of your business

In other words, what is your e-business? E-commerce can be divided into 7 types, from which it is certainly not difficult to choose the one that suits you best:

- Online only: the only way to see and buy goods is online;
- Mail orders: online sales and printed catalog (sometimes with one or two physical stores);
- Lots of bricks and clicks: lots of physical stores and one email. shop;
- Boutique Bricks and Clicks: One or two physical stores and e-mail shop;
- "Riding on a stranger's hump": Sales are made on Amazon or eBay platforms without having your e-mail. shops;
- Niche "riding on a stranger's hump": When sellers use group sales portals mainly (and regularly), sometimes with their email. shop;
- Fully multichannel: multiple email shops, catalogs, and e-commerce are the most complicated and difficult to manage e-businesses.

Identify your sales strengths

Make sure everything (both sellers and buyers) is clear. If you read that your strength is customer service, then make sure that the customer can always contact you.

Don't try to sell everything on the very first day

Most successful e-shops sell a certain category of goods. Find your niche to target your business. If you have goals and a target audience (target niche), your business can become much more successful because:

- It is easy for customers to understand your business. If customers understand your business, they will most likely recommend you and visit you regularly.

- It gives you more experience in purchasing (or manufacturing) certain goods.

- Easier financial control. You know that if you buy X quantity, you will sell in Y time. At the same time - no need to make huge purchases and investments.

- Marketing becomes easier. Generally, you need to choose one message that is well understood by your customers and promote it.

- It's easy to become an expert in your field. Why isn't Sony the best hardware? Why aren't the best cameras from Panasonic? Because these manufacturers realize themselves in a great many areas. Manufacturers like Focal (car speaker manufacturers) cannot afford to produce bad goods because they only work in that field and negative feedback ruins the whole business. By trading only certain goods - you will learn much more about them than sellers of "multifunctional stores" or ordinary buyers. You will be approached as an expert, asked for advice, and asked for help.

- Easy logistics. When you have the same goods - you know their sizes and weights, it is easy to negotiate with logistics service providers about delivery prices, it is easy to pack and send the goods.

Don't buy the wrong site

No matter how big or old your business is, your website must be relevant to the business and its goals. You have probably seen ads on the Internet (or in forums) that sell e-shops. I won't explain what to look for when buying an email. Store, but I will say this - no need to buy email. Stores for a five-digit amount when the products sold reach a three-digit amount in the first year.

Don't save on a website hosting plan

If your website is down or slow - customers will not buy anything from you. The fact that your position in search engines also depends on how fast your website works is also important.

Don't think that just because you have a website, visitors will buy something from you

Launching a website is not the same as opening a physical store. When you open a physical store, people are already walking on the sidewalk next to the store. This is not the case on the Internet.

Create a marketing plan

Even if it's only three months ahead - a marketing plan will help you focus your attention and promotional funds correctly where there is a return on investment.

Build a business with your strengths

If you have marketing experience - focus on marketing. If you have a vocation when writing - create amazing and engaging product descriptions. If you are a cool photographer - there is no doubt that the photos of the goods will be of enviable quality. Don't put your nose where you don't understand what you're doing. If you have hired professionals - do not interfere with their work. If you don't, ask for professional advice and listen to them.

Don't depend on just one marketing method

Diversity is needed to be successful. Leveraging your marketing experience and knowledge is a welcome thing, but no business has become successful with a single form of advertising. It is recommended to have at least three or four types of marketing - email. email, public relations, social networks, blogs, PPC advertising, video advertising, regular mail, etc.

Always try to collect customer data

Yes, it sounds tragic and manic. However, customer data is not intended to be sold to Tele2 or Bite so that their agents can then call them and offer what they cannot do on their own. On the first day, you don't think a greeting card can improve sales, but when the day comes and you realize that, it will be too late because you won't have to send those cards. To collect data from day one.

Integrate Google Analytics into your website code

Don't forget to fully program everything. I 'm talking about the conversion tracking feature. These data will be you in planning the second year. You're not going bankrupt, are you?

After completing the above - you will have much more than just an e-shop. You will have an e-business.

WHAT IS E-COMMERCE SEO?

E-commerce SEO is the process of making your online store more visible on search engine results pages (SERPs). When people are looking for the products you sell, you need to get as far ahead as possible to get more traffic.

You can get traffic from paid search (Google Ads), but SEO is cheaper. Besides, ad blockers and ad blindness can reduce the effectiveness of paid search.

E-commerce SEO typically involves optimizing your headlines, product descriptions, metadata, internal link structure, and navigation structure for search and user experience. Every product you sell should have a special page designed to drive traffic from search engines. But you should also keep in mind the static, non-product-oriented pages on your site, for example:

- Home Page
- About
- FAQ Page
- Blog Articles
- Contact Page

Create a list of keywords for these pages, as well as related keywords. You can use SEO audit tools such as Ahrefs, Ubersuggest, and SEMrush.

MODULE 16
LEAD GENERATION METHOD

What is a lead generation and how to generate a lead? How does lead generation work? How to generate leads? These are questions we get all the time. Before you start this lesson, let's start with the basics.

WHAT IS LEAD GENERATION?

In short, lead generation refers to the process of identifying potential customers for your business products or services. If you are a sales representative or a founder of a B2B company, you probably already have at least some experience in generating leads. Generating leads is not just a cold call or a plethora of emails. Sending letters, it is a complex process that requires a variety of strategies to be effective

In this lesson, we will explain what exactly the generation of potential customers means and describe some of the tactics for generating potential leads, which will increase your income.

WHAT IS LEAD?

A potential customer is a potential customer who has shown an interest in the services or products provided by your company. Their interest is expressed by sharing their contact information, such as email, phone number et.c.

WHY LEAD GENERATION MATTERS?

Lead is very important to both the marketing and sales team because it helps to:

- Get new sales samples
- Make the right wires

While acquiring potential customers essentially involves using both inbound and outbound tactics to generate leads, most sales reps and marketers find more success with inbound strategies.

WHAT IS MQL AND SQL?

- MQL - Marketing Qualified Leads
- SQL - Sales Qualified Lead

MQLs are perspectives that the marketing team considers promising but not yet ready to acquire - they have shown interest or made a connection, but they are not enough to determine their level of interest.

These examples are passed on to the marketing team, which then engages and nurtures them, providing relevant information, and evaluating potential customers based on their reactions and actions. When these potential buyers are deemed to be ready to buy, they are passed on to the sales team and become SQL.

The SQL domain determines which level of interest has been determined and has passed the engagement stage. They have been analyzed by both marketing and sales teams and they are already ready for the next stage of the process - direct sales. Each potential customer needs to be analyzed by both the sales team and the marketing team to determine where each customer is on the buyer's journey and how to approach them.

LEAD GENERATION CHANNELS

Not all lead generations are created equal. We will discuss the differences between incoming and outgoing channels and the specific channels in them and how they will cope with each other!

Outbound VS marketing is sent

There are two main channels for marketing leads:
- Outbound marketing
- Inbound marketing
-

If you don't know the 100% difference between an inbound and outbound, here's a quick breakdown:

Outbound marketing interrupts your client's workflow and "demands" their attention. Rather, inbound marketing attracts the customer to your channel and "grabs" his attention. Now that we have identified the main types of leads and identified the two main channels for generating leads.

HOW TO GENERATE CUSTOMER OR POTENTIAL LEADS?

A major shift in consumer attitudes towards advertising means that companies must adopt the tactics of their lead generation accordingly. You need to constantly check and implement new strategies to identify the ones that work for your company.

Here are some key points to look out for.

Has a website

If you don't have a website, it's almost impossible to establish an active online presence and attract targeted customers using natural traffic sources. However, with a website, you can provide valuable information to your target audience with compelling content and make sure your prospects always have a reason to come back.

Also, the site makes it easier to personalize the visitor experience and ensure that they see the most relevant information for them, depending on where they are visiting.

Make contact information visible and use the contact form

When designing your website, every decision must be made based on the potential customers you want to attract. You need to make browsing the site as easy as possible, and an important part is to put your contact information in a prominent place.

After all, attracting qualified customers to your site is an expensive and time-consuming process, so you can't risk losing them due to some insignificant form of contact information. And if you want to go a step further, you can even consider adding a chatbot or live chat feature to your site so that potential customers can reach you using the method that works best for them.

Use opt-out forms

Some of your visitors will not want to leave their contact information on your site unless they receive something of value. That's why it's so important to have a form of choice that allows you to capture potential customers and have an attractive incentive to leave their emails. The exact offer depends on your audience, but it needs to be valuable, such as a free trial or useful and effective information that they can use.

Direct pages and CTA

The landing page is an essential element of a successful lead generation strategy because it is where you capture customers by gathering their contact information.

The quality of your landing page will largely determine the success of the campaigns you manage, so to maximize your conversion rate, you need to spend as much time creating and editing it. Your landing pages should include a simple and clear message that highlights the value of the proposal and provides a basis for action. Try to remove any information that is not essential or irrelevant to your proposal, as this will only distract you and reduce your chances of success.

When creating your CTA (call to action), you need to make sure that they:

- Clear and understandable
- Forced
- Well, lead out on your website so that visitors can easily contact you.

Email Marketing

Even if you can make a visitor trust your email. An email address in exchange for a free trial or report doesn't mean it will automatically be interested in your product or even want to read your email. So it is no less important to create an email. An E-mail marketing campaign that would force readers to open your email. Letters and read them.

Your email Email addresses should provide the necessary information and foster prospects, directing them to the decision to purchase your product.

Retargeting

One way to increase every dollar you spend attracting new leads is to use redirect campaigns.
This means you shouldn't give up leadership just because he or she escaped from your site on your first visit. After all, he showed enough interest to be able to click first, so if you could interest him again in a slightly different message or special offer, you can see much better results.

Customer Referrals

If you can consistently provide great service to your customers, they will be much more likely to recommend you to their friends and colleagues, and this approval will make it easier to convert these shows. Because referrals are so valuable, you should actively seek them out and even consider encouraging your current customers by offering referral bonuses to every person they can bring you.

CHALLENGES FOR LEAD GENERATION

If they are pushing a product or solution that is not relevant or attractive to your potential customers, then they have no chance of making that sale. With that in mind, make sure you know your target audience like at your fingertips.

The right offer comes

Yes, you probably understand the key demographics of the people you want to target, including their.

- Age limits
- Gender
- Position / title
- Geographical position

- But that is not enough.

You should also know about your target customers

- Daily tasks
- Work-related objectives
- Work-related challenges
- KPIs and metrics
- Used publications and media

First of all, the area you want to focus on is your client's goals.

Many marketers tend to think that a customer's goals overlap with his company's sales goals, but your customer may have one or more secondary goals that they also want to achieve.

Suppose Company X has a revenue of $ 2,000,000 and the marketing director you are talking to is responsible for generating 500 customers to achieve that goal.

So, its main goal is to attract those customers - there is no doubt about that.

But once you get to know them better, they may also say that they have trouble justifying the marketing costs of the CFO, making it difficult for them to launch new campaigns and initiatives.

Bingo - You've just realized that their main goal is to find a way to more effectively calculate and report ROI for their campaigns.

So work on knowing your target audience from within, then use that knowledge to create a relevant and compelling offer for them.

Having enough people to generate customers

Here is the second most common challenge for lead generation:

Have enough people to generate leads.

If you encounter this problem, the solution is simple:

Stop generating wires manually and start automating the process.

Here are some lead generation tools that can help increase your productivity:

- AeroLeads
- Buffer
- LeadBoxer
- Marketo
- HubSpot
- Hoot Suite

With these tools, you can generate more qualified customers and increase sales.

Think about it: if lead generation methods are chosen manually, the number of your leads each month is limited by the number of your employees.

Assuming you are doing well when you need cash flow, a possible solution is to expand your team and hire more sales. But how fast can you grow? You are constrained by many factors, including your physical office space, as well as the speed your HR can hire and recruit new team members.

Measure the success of lead generation efforts

Finally, the third most common challenge faced by marketers is their generation. measuring the success of an effort. As management expert Peter Drucker says, if you can't measure, you can't improve it.

A tangible performance indicator makes it much easier to analyze the progress of your generation's efforts and make informed decisions in areas that need to be focused on.

Let's explore some of the key indicators you should look out for below.

- **Clickthrough rate (CTR)**

  PR indicates how compelling your call to action is.
  It also explains how to effectively move your customers using your funnel.
  The PR measurement formula is:
  CTR = total sales / total number of visitors * 100

  Wherever there is a CTA button, you should measure its PR.
  This applies not only to websites and landing pages but also to PPC ads and email. For mail campaigns.

- **Conversion rate**

  The conversion rate indicates how many visitors take action, such as filling out a form or making a purchase.
  The formula for measuring the conversion factor is as follows:
  Conversion rate = total sales / number of unique visitors * 100

  B2B marketers are offered the most important conversion rates:

  - Visitors lead
  - Leads to an opportunity ("opportunity" means a potential customer who is referred to a sales team)
  - Possibility to close
  - If you need to increase your site's conversion rate, check out this MixBloom article.

- **Time turns**

  This explains how long it takes for a visitor to turn into a verified guide.
  If you sell a more expensive high-end product or software, a potential buyer may spend more time browsing through your site before they become a potential buyer.
  Assuming you have a complicated approval or qualification process, this can also extend your conversion time (specifically from visitor to primary).

  Here is the time conversion formula:

  Total time spent by all visitors / Total number of potential customers

  By tracking conversion time, you can more accurately predict the length of your sales cycle.

  This will help you anticipate the number of potential customers you need to generate and prepare each month to reach your revenue goal by the end of the year.

- **Cost-per-click (CPC) and cost-per-mile (CPM)**

  If you're running any digital campaigns (Facebook and Google ads), you'll need to keep a close eye on the costs involved.
  If you pay for each click you receive, this is a CPC. If you pay per mile (thousand impressions), this is CPM.

Here are the relevant formulas:
CPC = advertising cost / clicks
CPM = cost / (impressions / 1000)
The lower the CPC and CPM, the better.

But, If one of your campaigns is constantly generating leads that later turn into customers with a high customer life expectancy (CLV), that's another story. Because you earn more revenue from these potential customers, it's great to continue to receive them, even if they have a higher CPC or CPM.

Effort and invest more time and money into strategies with the highest ROI.

MODULE 17
ONLINE REPUTATION MANAGEMENT

WHAT IS ONLINE REPUTATION?

It is the perception of people, whether they are customers or potential customers about your business. Everyone has an opinion about your brand and those opinions form your reputation. The reputation of a local business is primarily expressed by the reviews it receives on online review sites. The content of social media is a fundamental factor in influencing the formation of the perception of that company in the consumer's mind.

The role of online reputation management is to ensure that only the best content about your company appears to the consumer and thus influences the purchase decision in your favor.

WHY DO ONLINE REPUTATION MANAGEMENT?

Online reputation management is critical for companies to maintain positive brand identity in the views of consumers.

- Actively managing your reputation helps you to
- Influence customers' perceptions of your business
- Improve your visibility on the Internet
- Influence purchasing decisions in your favor

People don't know you when they visit your website, looking for places to stroll, eat, buy, or hire a service. If you have a good reputation, customers will show an interest in you. On the other hand, a negative or doubtful image is a great repellent for customers.

DO YOU CONTROL THE ONLINE REPUTATION OF YOUR BUSINESS?

You have no control over what people say about you on the web, but that doesn't mean you can't be influential. And that is exactly where online reputation management comes in.

Reputation management is the effort to influence what people think about a brand. The part of the reputation you control corresponds to the content you share on the web, the ads, partnerships, service, in short. However, even so, you are not in control of how this will be perceived, because the perception of business develops independently and individually in each person's mind.

However, this does not prevent you from managing your business' online presence. Although you can adjust what people see about you online to some extent, you can't control what they think, and for that reason, management is limited.

The manager's role will be to influence how people perceive their business and prevent or minimize negative results that harm the business image. Managing does not mean you will never see negative content about your business on the web again. However, with efficient management, these contents will have less impact on your business.

HOW YOUR BUSINESS ONLINE REPUTATION IS BUILT?

Investing in your online reputation will bring you more results in the long run than any advertising campaign. This is because you will be building the image of your business, a legacy of trust and credibility that, it worked well, will become one of the most important assets of your business.

The following are the main points addressed in building a solid and positive reputation:

Customer Experience

The basis for an excellent reputation is investing in the customer experience. You do this by setting your customers' expectations and then setting how to exceed them.

Identity of your business

What do you promise? How are you different from your competitors? What values do you stand for? What is your history? A well-told story can be a great asset in your favor. Are you a company that promises a luxurious experience or one that guarantees quality at an affordable price?

Online presence

Just a profile on Facebook and you already have an online presence, however, this is not enough for the market. We need more information about you. Your online reputation is built on the content found about your company on the web. The more positive (and honest) content, the better.

Reviews

Reviews directly impact the perception of your company. It is the first thing that consumers look at. Your reputation will be perceived according to the sentiment of these online reviews.

ASSESSING YOUR BUSINESS ONLINE REPUTATION

By measuring and understanding your reputation, we can:
- Understand which areas of your business work well.
- Be aware of which areas present a reputation risk.
- Predict the actions that your stakeholders will take.

- Identify opportunities to drive business success.

SIGNS THAT YOUR BUSINESS HAS A GOOD REPUTATION ONLINE

- Accurate results in a google search.
- Most of the content that appears is positive.
- You have a score above 4.
- Recent and commented reviews.
- The low number of negative reviews.
- The great majority of answered reviews.
- Active participation in your social profiles.
- Your company appears in the top positions in a survey about your niche.

SIGNS THAT YOUR BUSINESS HAS A NEGATIVE REPUTATION ONLINE

- Inaccurate search results - find nothing or insignificant information about your company in a Google search.
- Many negative comments.
- Content with inappropriate language.
- The high volume of unanswered reviews.
- The most recent review is over two weeks old.
- Incomplete information about your business.
- Abandoned social profiles.

HOW TO ASSESS YOUR COMPANY'S ONLINE REPUTATION?

For this, you will do a vast search in search of content about your company available on the web. Follow these steps:

- **General search:** pretend you're a customer looking for what your business offers, type in your keywords, and hit enter. See if: your business appeared in the results; in what position did he appear; and who is in the first place.

- **Specific search:** type the name of your establishment on Google and take note of the results that appear on the first page. Search for all terms related to your brand, including product names, hashtags, slogans, or any other meaningful term for your brand identity.

- **In-depth search:** now you will look at the reviews, comments, reviews you received in the last month on review sites, social networks. Also, evaluate the engagement promoted by you. What is the prevailing feeling?

- **Competitor Search:** Search for your top competitors on Google. Read and rate your reviews. Who has the most positive feeling? Who is more engaged? Who appears in the first results?

The second phase is to evaluate these data more deeply. Try to answer the questions below and, in the end, you will have an image of the situation your company's reputation is in.

- What is the general feeling of your brand? And what is the result compared to that of your competitors (better, little better, worse, etc.)?
- How do you feel about your online assessments? Your average star rating?
- What positively influenced your reputation? Actions, strategies, partnerships, etc.
- Which competitors have the strongest reputation?
- What can you do to achieve similar results?
- Which social media channels were most influential in building a positive reputation?
- What kind of information needs to be published on social media to influence a positive reputation?
- What negative information is damaging your reputation?

REVIEW- HOW MUCH THEY IMPACT YOUR BUSINESS ONLINE REPUTATION

Reading negative reviews means that 40% of consumers do not want to use a local company. If you invest in generating positive reviews it will improve your reputation and people will prefer to choose you over your competitor. Although obvious, very few companies are investing in generating reviews.

Reviews are the first thing the consumer looks at before deciding whether a deal is good or not, that's a fact. They pay attention if they are recent, the volume of reviews of the company, the general score, and if you answer them.

Next, I'll tell you how to manage reviews properly to maintain a strong and positive reputation in 4 steps:

Review sites

Google and Facebook have become number 1 and number 2 for online reviews. So, if you don't already have a profile on these platforms, do it now.

Receive reviews

Having a constant flow of evaluations is essential. In addition to serving as an excellent social proof for future clients, they are a powerful source of inputs to identify problems and opportunities.

Reply

As important as receiving reviews, you must respond to them. When customers are answered, perceptions improve immediately. 80% of consumers believe that a company cares more about them when their reviews are answered.

Monitor

You cannot control what they say about you, but you can and should monitor that content. Monitoring allows you to be proactive in identifying possible crises and opportunities. The Google Alert is a tool that notifies you whenever your brand is mentioned on the web, and you can set it to alert you about various terms that you want, including over its competitors.

SOCIAL MEDIA – HOW MUCH IT IMPACTS YOUR COMPANY'S ONLINE REPUTATION

First of all, understand social media as all user-generated content. In other words, people themselves create, share, and consume the content generated by themselves. Where do we find this content? on blogs, on YouTube, Twitter, Facebook, review sites, forums, they are all social media platforms, as they allow the creation and sharing of content produced by the user. With more and more people turning to social media to find out about local businesses, these companies must manage and monitor their online presence. Online word-of-mouth, references, reviews, and an established network of regular customers help to increase the visibility and reputation of a local company.

Here's a simple, 3-step formula on how to manage social media to optimize your business's online reputation:

Configure

- **Define the platforms**
  There is a multitude of them available, each varying in content format, audience, and functionality. Choose the ones that best suit your business needs.

- **Adjust the Contact Information**
  Always keep your contact information complete (name, address, location, telephone, etc.). Take advantage of the biography/description space to present your company.

- **Set a Routine**
  Establish a routine of interactions. I'm not telling you to post every day, 3x a day, but to be consistent in publishing content.

Engage

- Share useful content that delivers value. No clogging your feed saying how much betters your product/service is then your competitor. Limit promotional content to 20% of all content you share. The rest you focus on offering engaging content, such as tips, curiosities, news, news, or humor.

- Be personal and authentic. Let the human side flourish; it makes the user feel that there is a real person behind that publication. Start by setting your tone of voice: relaxed, serious, or formal.

- The conversation is a two-way street, so respond whenever possible to your audience's interactions.

Measure

- Review your strategies and metrics. Evaluate your performance and make the necessary changes.

HOW TO PROTECT YOUR COMPANY'S ONLINE REPUTATION

As the saying goes, "prevention is better than cure". And when it comes to reputation, something that we have limited management, prevention is always the best alternative. For this reason, we will start by talking about monitoring.

Monitoring: a key to maintaining a positive reputation

It is in the monitoring phase that most problems are avoided. Negative content is like fire on dry grass, it spreads quickly and light takes on huge proportions if you don't stop it, as long as it's just a fire.

Set a schedule that will accompany the reviews and their social profiles. Rate this content and respond as much as you can. At least once a month, have a meeting with your team.

Cover your monitoring for the entire market. Follow the main problems and trends that can affect your business. Also, keep an eye on the steps of your business partners.

Competitors' reputations also need to be monitored. Is it your company or theirs that is getting the most conversations week by week? Remember, if a company has the best perception, it is more likely to get the final sale.

Defining a plan for moments of crisis in online reputation

It is amazing how bad news gets there fast, so your response and position about the approaching storm must be just as fast. At first, the most important thing is to make it clear that you are aware of the problem and that you are doing everything possible to solve it.

Don't waste time writing or recording a great speech. A simple note on your website, Facebook, or twitter recognizing the problem and that soon you will make more information available, can already serve to calm the mood of the staff.

But be sure to provide updates on the situation over time. When taking action to correct your mistakes, publicize your actions on all channels you own. Regular and transparent communication with your audience is crucial.

HOW TO REPAIR A NEGATIVE REPUTATION

Imagine the following scenario: you pick up your phone and do a quick search for "best coffee in town" hoping to find your business on the search page. But, wait a minute, he didn't show up, all because some negative reviews that were written a few months ago. Well, in the eyes of Google, you have a negative reputation and are not worthy to appear in the top positions.

Or let's say that a scandal involving your company broke out right in your lap. Well, we already talked about the previous topic, how to act in times of crisis. Now I will show you how to act when you have a negative reputation.

Assess the size of the problem

When we have a problem to solve, what is the first thing we do? Understand the problem properly to have a full understanding of it. We will do the same thing with your negative online reputation.

Start with Google. See what you find about your company. Search by name, use keywords from your industry, search for your products, and everything else that has to do with your company. Visit the main review sites. Look for reviews about your business. Look at the complaint here.

Don't forget about social media, see what you find on Facebook, Instagram, or Twitter. Write down everything you find on a spreadsheet. You will have a better understanding of the size of your problem and where you should act first.

Creating a recovery plan

Once the dimension of the problem is understood, it is time to devise a resolution strategy. Rebuilding a damaged reputation is a content battle - waging a war on negative content and relentlessly publishing positive content, until "burying" negative content.

Set success indicators

Your goal is to reverse your negative reputation, but how do you know if you're going the right way? Establish "success indicators": number of reviews received during the week; the volume of grade 5 reviews, compared to grade 1 reviews; the percentage of reviews answered in 7 days.

Start responding

Do you know all those negative results you found in your problem recognition research? You need to answer all of them. Start with the most serious and most recent. And take the conversation offline by offering a phone number or email.

Some people will prefer to continue the discussion in the public, the bright side is that you have found that it is not where you should invest your efforts to improve your reputation.

Acting on the problem

So, if your negative reputation is the result of a scandal, you already know what the problem needs to be tackled. However, if you still don't know, take a deep look at your reviews and find the main points raised by your customers, both positive and negative. The negatives you should seek to correct immediately. As for the positives, you should reinforce them even more, and use them to your advantage by highlighting them in your media on the web. And remember to express your commitment to change to your audience.

Communicate effectively

The worst thing you can do when you are experiencing a problem, as in a scandal, that hurts the integrity of your brand, is to play dumb and deaf as if nothing is happening. Your attitude should be to assume that something has gone wrong and that you are willing to do your best. We already talked about this in the crisis topic.

Content production

Remember that I mentioned that rebuilding a damaged reputation is a content battle? Your next step should be to produce and disseminate positive content about your company: it is worth positive reviews, improvements in the establishment, promises you are willing to keep to deliver the best experience, an event you participated in, and prizes, everything that can push the negative content from the 1st to google page for page 2 onwards. Attention: share valuable content, content that will interest consumers.

Investing in the customer experience

Make sure that you serve your customers in the same way that you would like to be served and try to exceed their expectations. Get your team together and start creating a culture that puts customer experience at the center of business strategy.

Put your review generation plan into practice

The reputation of a local business is formed by reviews. If your rating is low, if you have few reviews, implement a review generation plan. Not only do they not improve your rank on Google, but they also offer powerful inputs on what needs to be improved in your customer's experience.

Delete negative web results

So, wouldn't it be a lot easier to erase all that negative result and have a brand-new spotless reputation? Well, that is not possible. Our legislation does not oblige the online content provider to be responsible for the content published there and for that reason, it has no duty or obligation to remove anything. In some specific cases, the company does get a court order for the content to be removed. But it can be an exhausting and time-consuming process. The best way to "remove" negative content from the web is to "bury" it under a heap of positive content.

HOW TO KEEP YOUR ONLINE REPUTATION HIGH?

Now that everything is ok with the online reputation of your business, you want it to stay that way, correct? Here are some practices for you to follow and keep your reputation going:
- Monitor your reviews regularly;
- Keep your social profile information up to date;
- Share your positive reviews;
- Be active and try to engage your audience on social media;
- Always be kind and polite in your interactions;
- Your number 1 page on google is your calling card. Make sure that all the information that appears here benefits your business.
- Invest in good design for your pages.
- Think about hiring someone specialized in the area, even if your internal team is a top 10, a professional can do wonders for your company.

BUILD AN ONLINE REUTATION STRATEGY FOR YOUR BUSINESS

Search

Search for your company and everything related to it on google, on social networks, on reputable sites, in your customer service sector. At this point, you need to understand what the feeling is about your company. Take note of all the results. Also, search for influencers and your main competitors. Also, do the same search using an anonymous tab in your browser, so the results will not be influenced by your browsing history.

Rate

Once you have the information acquired in the previous phase, you will evaluate it in more depth. Remember we talked about how to make that assessment up there.

Identify strengths

The time has come to identify your strengths in terms of reputation. These are the points where you should focus your efforts to obtain more expressive results in managing your reputation. Look at your strengths and see what you can replicate or expand. See also how to use this force to reverse a negative point.

Identifying weaknesses

Just as you identified your strengths, also spot your weaknesses. Identify your vulnerable points and prioritize strengthening those with the highest risk potential.

Imitate success

In your list of main competitors, do you have one with a stronger reputation than yours? Or some strategy that he has been implementing that presents very good results and that you could use the idea? The same thinking holds for companies in markets that differ from yours. Select the one (s) that have a reputation with the best result and choose the best ideas.

Content

Finally, content. To have an online reputation, you need to have content about it. It will be through the content found online that consumers will form their opinion about your company. This content comes mainly in the form of online reviews and social media. Your company producing or not producing content, it will exist. So, define a strategy that further strengthens your reputation

MODULE 18
REMARKETING AND RETARGETING

REMARKETING AND RETARGETING

There are two points of view on the difference between remarketing and retargeting.

Remarketing is an advertising strategy whose goal is to keep the attention of potential customers who have expressed interest in the brand.

Retargeting is a technology for displaying ads to users whose behavior meets predefined conditions. For example, they went to the site and added goods to the basket, clicked on the banner, liked the post, or filled out the form on the landing page.
In this case, the main difference between remarketing and retargeting is that the first concept is wider and includes the second. Like "fruit" and "apple": remarketing will be a strategy for returning a user to the site, and retargeting will be a return tool separately in each advertising system.

But other experts say that there is no difference: just in some advertising systems, technology is called remarketing, and in others - retargeting, that's all.
However, different approaches to definitions do not affect the operation of the technology. But the action plan is needed, whatever you call it.

HOW DOES RETARGETING WORK?

Retargeting shows ads to those who have already contacted you. I visited your site, saw a YouTube commercial, and liked posts on VK, and so on. Such an audience is called "warm" and is considered the most conversive, so retargeting is an essential part of digital marketing in any company.

Especially effective technology is used in two types of areas:

- Spheres with an average and long purchase cycle (real estate, cars, etc.) - users who are in the process of choosing and making decisions see ads. Retargeting allows you to "warm-up" them and brings them to purchase faster.
- Spheres with rapidly renewable demand (food, beauty services, etc.) - here you need to take into account the length of the purchase cycle and show ads in anticipation of the new. For example, girls do manicure once every 4 weeks, you can show them ads 3 weeks after the visit to prevent them from leaving for another studio.

Settings for collecting retargeting audiences and launching an advertising campaign are made in the office of the selected site.

HOW RETARGETING WORKS

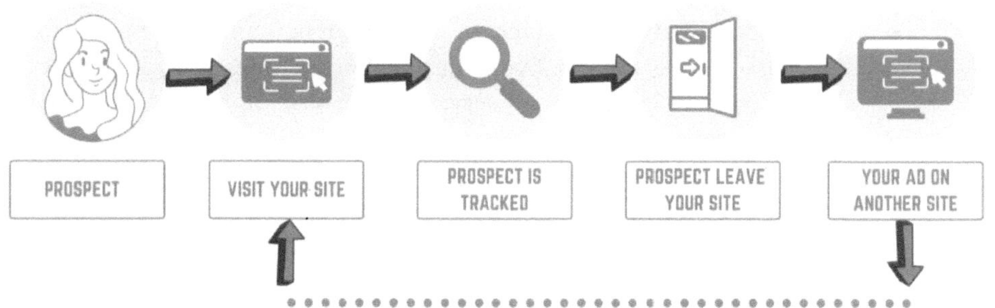

RETARGETING SOLUTIONS

- The user went to the site, looked and left, while he did not leave a request, but showed his interest: visited several pages or looked at a section for a long time. The task is to return the user so that he performs the target action. A special offer will come in handy here, which will further motivate a potential client - after all, for the first time, he still left. Or useful content that warms it up:
- The user is already your client: he made purchases earlier and now you want to talk about new products or he registered for the event, and now you spend one more and so on - all possible additional sales.
- Abandoned basket. The classic script for e-commerce. You can attach a link to the basket with the goods that the user added. Or set up dynamic ads with product cards that interest him.

- Return after display advertising: if the user has not yet seen your site, but watched the video until some point or saw the banners several times. Here you can show the user a personalized offer that will advance him further along the funnel.

RETARGETING TYPES

- **Standard remarketing** - advertising is shown on the specified segments of visitors to your site.

- **Search** - is shown only in search engines.

- **Dynamic** - users who viewed certain pages of the site see dynamic creatives. They have generated automatically in real-time based on data that is known about the user. This type of retargeting allows you to show the most personalized offer.

- **Product (content)** - a kind of dynamic retargeting. A "product feed" is a data source for creatives - a list that includes images, prices, and descriptions of products or services. The user in the ad will see only what he was interested in.

- **CRM retargeting** - focused on cross-selling. Based on the information about purchases made, the current customers are offered related products in the ads.

- **Cross-device** - allows you to show ads on different devices of the user, even if he came to your site from only one of them.

RETARGETING METHODS

Retargeting and remarketing are configured in different ways and each of them gives their unique opportunities. Let's take them apart.

Website visitors retargeting

Where can I run: Google Ads, Yahoo, Facebook, and Instagram, myTarget.

What it gives: you can show ads to users who have performed a given action on the site - from viewing the page to clicking the button. Or simply gather specific website visitors into one segment to display ads targeted specifically to them:

In this case, you will have to add a web analytics counter or a special pixel to the code of your site that will transmit information about user actions on your site to advertising desks.

In Google Ads, Bing such retargeting is launched through synchronization of advertising accounts with web analytics counters: Bing analytics, Google Analytics, and Top.mail.ru, respectively. They allow you to create segments of the audience by the behavior on the site. Social networks have their pixels for this.

Retargeting the uploaded list of numbers and email addresses of your customers

Where can I run: Google Ads, Yahoo, Facebook, and Instagram, myTarget.

What gives: you can launch an audience for those who were interested in your product, but did not buy it, or vice versa - exclude from the display those who are already your customers.

The download file must be in CSV format and contain data in a specific format. This data can be obtained from your CRM or any other system in which you store customer contact information. Next, the file will have to be assembled by hand. Although there are exceptions.

Display Targeting Retargeting

Where to start: YouTube (through Google Ads), Yandex, myTarget.

What it gives: you can take funnel to a new level of users who have already seen your display ads but have not moved to the site.

Display advertising is used for outreach purposes so that the brand and its product are fixed in the head of the audience. This works with video ads, contextual search banners and even outdoor advertising.

On YouTube, it works: you can show ads to users who have watched any video on your channel or a specific video. To do this, you need to link your YouTube account and Google Ads. See the Google manual for instructions on how to do this. Remarketing itself, as well as advertising on YouTube, is configured through Google Ads.

Retargeting the actions of the audience on your pages on social networks

Where to start: Facebook, Instagram, VKontakte, myTarget.

What gives: you can show additional advertising to users who interacted with your content on social networks.

In Social media, you can set retargeting for those who interacted with your advertising record: like, commented, reposted. There is no way to set retargeting for those who organically interacted with your posts, but this audience can be assembled with the help of parsers (however, it is already difficult to call it retargeting).

YOU CAN RETARGET THOSE WHO:

- Reacted to your event on Facebook,
- Visited the Facebook page,
- Interacted with any post, including advertising: left a reaction, comment, reposted, clicked on a link or flipped through a ring gallery,
- Who pressed the call to action button
- Who wrote in private messages Pages,
- Saved post or page.
- In terms of Instagram business profile, you can choose:
- Everyone who visited your business profile, even if these users didn't take any action,
- Only those who like, comment on any post or advertisement, click on a button or otherwise interact with your post,
- Only those who wrote Direct messages to your business profile,
- Those who have retained any of your posts or announcements.

MODULE 19
GOOGLE ADSENSE

GOOGLE ADSENSE

What it is, how it works and how to use it on Youtube

In this lesson, learn how you can use Google AdSense to make money on the internet and how to receive your payments from Google!

Google AdSense is an advertising platform that allows Google to place ads on your blog, website, videos, applications, and more. Understand more about the tool and how to use it. Making money on the internet is becoming very common; it means that the trend for the future is professions performed entirely through digital media. A good option for you is Google AdSense, which allows you to bill with your channel on YouTube.

In exchange for inserting ads in content posted on YouTube, Google pays the website owner the "rent" for that space, also paying for the number of clicks, impressions, and more. If you want to make the pleasure of using the internet in a successful business, check out in this article how you can use Google AdSense to make money on the internet and how to receive your payments from Google!

WHAT IS GOOGLE ADSENSE?

AdSense is a tool developed by Google that allows the owner of a YouTube channel, blog, or website to profit from third party ads in their communication medium, doing strategic marketing that benefits everyone.

When a company wants to advertise its brand by digital means, AdSense places the ad on the YouTube video of those who are registered and for each click made by followers on the content you posted, Google passes a percentage to your account.

WHAT ARE THE WAYS TO MAKE MONEY ON YOUTUBE?

There are possibilities to make money on YouTube in different ways, however, each resource has its particularities, requirements, and minimums that are established and evaluated by Google.

If a channel does not meet the·specifications and requirements, it is not possible to activate the features and start making money. The main ways to profit from YouTube are:

- **Advertising:** Revenue generated by the placement of ads overlaid on the video
- **Channel Products:** sale of official brand products disclosed in the publication;
- **YouTube Premium:** Revenue generated when a YouTube premium user watches your content;
- **Channel Club:** whoever uses your channel pays for possible benefits created and offered by you.

WHAT ARE THE REQUIREMENTS FOR ENABLING CHANNEL MONETIZATION ON YOUTUBE?

Each resource has its requirements for monetization and as soon as it is accepted into the program, it must be analyzed according to the medium it chooses to earn money. The requirements for each form are as follows:

- **Advertising:** being over 18 or having a person responsible for managing payments and following the rules for adequate content.
- **Channel Products:** have more than 10,000 subscribers on the channel and are 18 years old or older.
- **YouTube Premium:** develop content that is watched by YouTube premium customers.
- **Channel Club:** have more than 30 thousand subscribers and be over 18 years old.

WHAT DOES IT TAKES TO HAVE A GOOGLE ADSENSE ACCOUNT?

There are no secrets to signing up for AdSense: just a Google email account (Gmail), your website, a phone number, and your address. Anyone of legal age can generate revenue on your site using the service, as long as your site complies with company rules, that is, it does not contain prejudiced content that incites violence or sexual content.

How do I sign up?

The process to sign up is simple and doesn't require much, but you need to be careful because to use AdSense, you need to have your domain. Sites hosted on subdomains are not accepted in this partnership.

After entering the information, Google performs an inspection to confirm that the site fits the terms of use of the platform. To sign up, just follow simple steps, such as:

- Access the service page;
- Enter the email you will use in your profile;
- Fill in the requested information: name of the blog, country of origin, and terms of use.

Stay tuned: ads will start showing only after this check!

The last step in the Google AdSense registration process is to enter your account details to receive the money. Since Google is an American company, payment is made in dollars, once a month.

This payment is only released when it reaches a minimum profit, usually one hundred dollars. In addition to the quote, it is very important to check the rates applied by your bank to receive payments from abroad; they can already reach high percentages of the total value.

One of the best-known options on the market charges twenty dollars for each receipt, which consumes a large part of small payments.

Can I live on the income earned from AdSense profits?

Before you drop everything and decide to live off ads on your site, know that the income varies according to the theme of your site, the number of advertisers in your niche, the number of visitors, the reach of your publications, the quality of the content and much more.

To live on digital content, it is important to strategize your business, know how much you can invest until you start to profit and much more.

What types of ads does Google AdSense offer?

Google has thousands of partners and divides ads into categories. Within the tool, it is possible to insert several text ads (sponsored links, titles, and posts), image ads (banners), link units, and the so-called rich media, special and interactive ads such as gifs, videos and HTML creations.

Google has thousands of partners and divides ads into categories. Within the tool, it is possible to insert several text ads (sponsored links, titles, posts), image ads (banners), link units, and the so-called rich media, special and interactive ads such as gifs, videos and HTML creations.

It is possible to place several ads on your page, however, if Google understands that they do not make sense or do not add value to the reader, the company can limit the number of ads, or even disable them. The most used types of ads consist of:

- **Video Ads:** pinned to strategic locations and can be seen throughout the video display;
- **Image Ads:** are like banners and displayed on the entire page during the video;
- **In-Stream:** Short marketing video that passes before the video selected by the user is shown;
- **TrueView:** Ads that appear in the corners or below, when the person searches for a video on YouTube.

It is possible to place several ads on your page; however, if Google understands that these do not make sense or do not add value to the reader, the company can limit the number of ads, or even disable them.

HOW TO USE GOOGLE ADSENSE ON YOUTUBE?

We talk a lot about websites and blogs, but a very large audience is the creators of content for Youtube. Vloggers, gamers, specialized channels, and all kinds of digital influencers use Google's video platform to create their works.

With that in mind, AdSense is also available for YouTube, which can be activated as simply as on the website. To run your YouTube account on AdSense just follows the step by step below.

Click the option to set up AdSense on YouTube

The first step is to click on the option to set up AdSense on the channel and access the registration page for the platform. Enter your data and e-mail, also bank information. Once it is all filled in properly, submit the form, which will be analyzed by Google.

Enable Monetization

After entering your channel and activating the monetization option (available in the "Creator Studio" menu), you can create an AdSense account for your channel or link to an existing account like your website, for example.

Accept the request and post videos

The next step is to accept the request and post your videos. Always remember that for a video to be monetized, it must be free of copyright, that is, do not use third party content without the permission of the original creators.

Understand how to find your AdSense earnings

The first mistake made by many YouTubers in AdSense is to believe that you will monetize immediately, however, it is essential to follow the performance reports and understand the entire process to receive, since the amounts are paid in dollars and an international transaction is essential.

MODULE 20
GOOGLE ANALYTICS: THE COMPLETE GUIDE

In this lesson, you will read indications, secrets, and tricks on one of the most powerful web marketing tools. You will find out how to use Google Analytics to monitor professional sites, company sites, and e-commerce. This lesson is designed for beginners but also the more expert pinch. So, are you ready? Let's find out how Google Analytics works!

WHAT IS GOOGLE ANALYTICS?

If you believe that Google Analytics only serves to monitor access to your website, you are wrong. GA is, first of all, a very powerful web marketing tool through which to analyze digital data, or information deriving from your online strategies. Study the behavior of users of your site, check which channels or campaigns work, which do not, and eventually correct the errors.
Google Analytics is therefore useful:

- `To publishers, to refine strategies for engaging their audiences.
- To e-commerce owners or professionals, to understand which products or services sell the most and through which channels.
- To those who deal with lead acquisition, to put potential sellers and leads in contact.

HOW TO MONITOR A WEBSITE: THE ANALYTICS CODE

How does Google Analytics work? Google Analytics can monitor a website through the installation of a simple tracking code. This code is in JavaScript language and controls the entire website: as soon as a user visits a page, the code (or snippet) anonymously collects the information and sends it to Google Analytics.

How to get the tracking code?

To get the tracking code, you need to create a Google Analytics account. How? Easy: follow these step-by-step instructions!

- Log in to your Google Account (if you don't have one, create it).
- Access the Google Analytics home page.
- Click on the "Register" button.
- Set the name of your account, indicate the URL of the website, the category it belongs to, and a time zone.
- Click on the "Get Tracking ID" button at the bottom of the page, and the code will be yours.

How the tracking code works: reports and sessions

What information does the Analytics code collect? The data related to traffic sources (search engines, social, etc.), The browser (the language, the type), the device and the operating system used, and more.

Analytics groups this data into reports i.e. reports on the use of the site that exploits different metrics (the device used, the country of origin, etc.). User activities, however, are organized into sessions. Be careful not to confuse a session with viewing a page:

Enter the tracking code on the site

You can enter the Google Analytics tracking code on your site in three ways:

- Manually, by copying and pasting the snippet into the site header (before the </head> tag)

- Through Google Tag Manager (an interesting option, which we will see soon in an ad hoc article!)

- Through a plugin, if your site is made with a CMS (for example, WordPress)

In the latter case, I highly recommend the Google Analytics for WordPress by MonsterInsights plugin. It is an extremely simple and powerful solution!

Google Analytics configuration

A self-respecting Google Analytics guide cannot fail to provide an overview of the optimal organization and the constitutive elements of this powerful tool. Before embarking on the analysis of the reports, let's find out how to best configure Analytics!

Accounts, properties, views

When you create an account, the property is also automatically generated in Google Analytics (the website you are monitoring) and, within the latter, a view (i.e. a set of rules for displaying data). An account can manage multiple properties: this means that if you are, for example, a web marketing professional and you have many customers, with a single account you can access the reports of multiple websites. Each property, in turn, can have multiple views.

What is the use of having multiple views? For example, you could use single views to monitor specific areas of the site (in case you have a large site and need to monitor the various sections in more depth). Or to exclude from your reports the traffic generated by bots and spiders known to Google and maybe even internal traffic (i.e. access to your or your employees' site).

The latter case is perhaps the most frequent for small and medium-sized sites: let's see how to proceed!

Set up basic views

From the initial Google Analytics screen, go to Administration > select the property you are interested in working on and, in the right column, click on "View settings".

The basic view of Google Analytics is called "All website data": rename it to "Raw data" and save. After that:

- Click on the arrow at the top left and return to the Administration screen;
- In the right column, click on the "+Creat View".
- Give it the name "Test View", select the correct country and time zone and click on "Create view" ;
- Go to the "View settings" of the new view and check the box "Exclude all hits from known bots and spiders" ;
- Save;

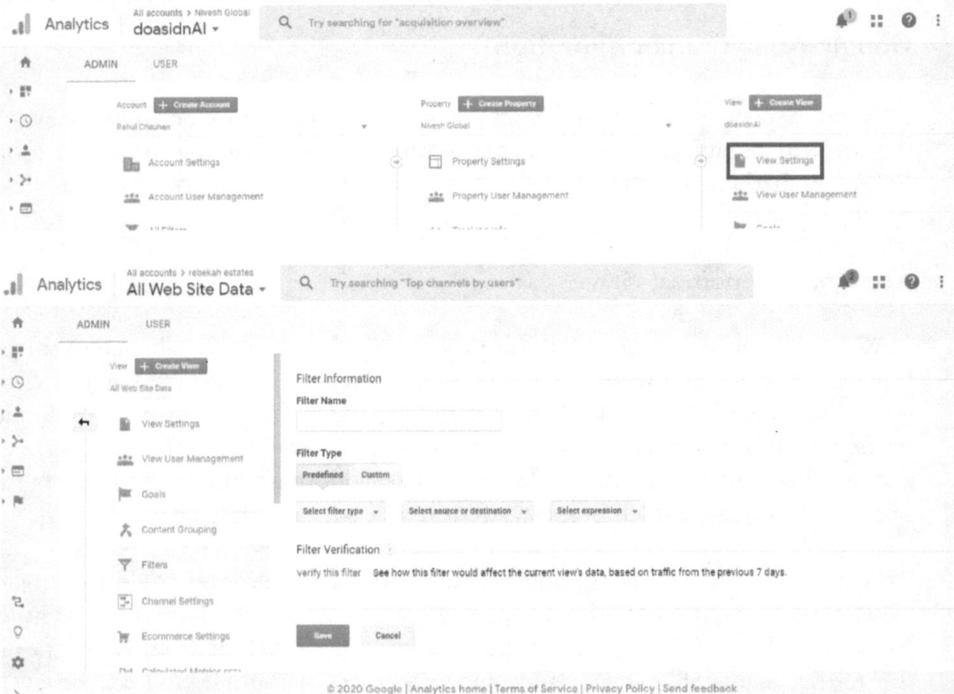

The test view is used to test the data and to be sure that there are no errors in the data display. It will take a few hours for the "Test View" to collect the data. As soon as it is checked for correctness, select it in the "View" column and click on "View settings". At the top right you have the "Copy view" button: give the new view the name "Main view".

Now we need to apply a filter to the "Test View" to exclude the traffic generated by your IP.

- From the menu of the "View" column go to Filters> Add Filters . Give a name to the filter (eg "Internal traffic"); on "Select the type of filter" choose "Exclude"; on "Select a source or a destination" choose "Traffic of IP addresses" and on "Select an expression" select "Same as".
- Enter your IP address in the field below. You can get it from this tool: http://whatismyipaddress.com; finally save.

Again, wait a few hours to verify that the view is working properly (you will find that it works if your reports do not show traffic anomalies). After that, it also applies the filter to the main view. That's how:

- In the "View" column, select "The main view" and click on Filters> Add Filters> Apply Existing Filters: select the "Internal traffic" filter, which will thus be applied to the view.

In this way you will have two views: a "raw" ("Raw data", in fact) which will contain all the data, and a "filtered" ("Main view") which will exclude internal traffic and that of known bots and spiders to Google. To put it with a chart:

To delete a view, just select it in the drop-down menu, click on "View settings" and from there on the button at the top right, "Move to trash". The view will be permanently deleted by Google after 35 days.

User permissions

On the "Administration" page, you will notice how the Account, Properties, and Views columns have all three options: "User management". It means that with Google Analytics you can share Accounts, Properties, and Views, or allow other users to access them.

So Click on the button, enter the email (obviously Gmail) of the user with whom you want to share information and establish the permissions (if you want the user to be able to read or make changes or maybe add other users in turn). Keep in mind that:

- If you share an Account, whatever the functions you attribute to it, the user will be able to analyze the data of all the properties of that account (and of course the related views).

- If you share a property, however, the user will have access to the data of that one Property (and its Views): he will not see the other Properties.

- If you share a View, however, the user will be able to analyze only the data of the View in question, not the other views of that Property, the Property itself or the Account.

How Google Analytics is made

Let's start warming up the engines: this section of "Google Analytics: the complete guide" shows you how the reports are structured, what are the basic metrics and how to organize the dashboards, to easily find all the data you want to keep an eye on!

The structure of relationships:

Google Analytics organizes data from user activity on your website into 5 reports:

- In real-time
- Public
- Acquisition
- Behavior
- Conversions

Each of these reports is based on different sets of metrics and is in turn divided into a variable number of reports, each of which relates to a specific dimension.

- The Audience reports provide information about users such as age and gender, geographic origin, etc.
- The Acquisition reports specify channels, sources, and means through which users come to your site.
- The Behavior reports indicate the most viewed pages, target pages, exit pages, etc.
- The reports conversions provide valuable information on the effectiveness of your campaigns.
- The Real-Time reports show the situation "live" on your site.

The reports show the data over a period which is by default set to the last seven days but can be varied.

Each of the 5 basic reports has an "Overview" section (also present in many secondary reports): it is the one in which the contents of the report are summarized through the reference metrics.

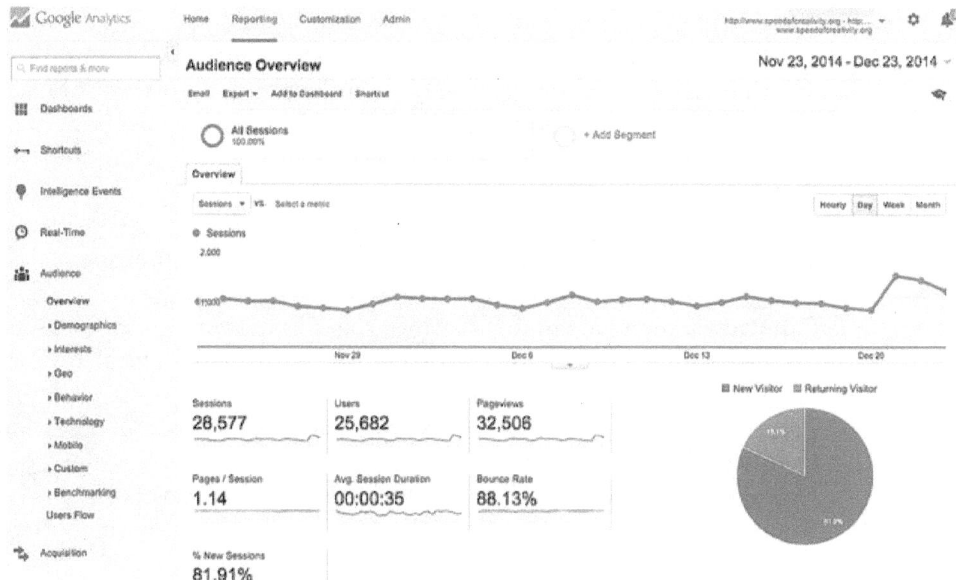

In more specific reports, in addition to the initial graph, you will find information organized in tables. Consider, for example, the report Local in Public> Geographical Data: the table shows the location of origin of the visitors of your site and the metrics of Acquisition, Behavior, and Conversions (we will see them very soon).

You need to know a few things about this table:

- You can click on the data relating to the main metric (in this case, the countries) to deepen the data. You can also sort the data in the columns in ascending or descending order simply by clicking on the column header.

- You can cross the "main dimension" (in this case, the location) with a "secondary dimension", to have as the first varies with the variation of the second. For example, you can select "device category" as a secondary dimension to understanding what type of device (pc, smartphone, tablet) users who connect to your site from various locations use.

- You can view the data not only in a table format but also with a pie chart, a performance chart, a comparison chart and with pivot mode: just click on the relative icons located above the table, on the right.

The basic metrics

Before analyzing the individual basic reports in detail and discovering their peculiarities, to understand how to use Google Analytics to improve your online communication, you must familiarize yourself with what are the most important metrics, i.e. those that appear in the Audience> Overview report. Here they are below:

- **Sessions:** the total number of sessions in the considered time interval;
- **Users:** the total number of visitors over a certain period;
- **Pageviews:** the total number of times pages have been viewed by users. Attention, these are not "unique views": the data includes repeated views of a single page by the same user;
- **Pages per session:** the average number of pages viewed in a session (repeated page views are included);
- **Average session duration:** how long a session lasts on average;
- **Bounce rate:** measures how many users have left after viewing a page and have not taken any further action.

Dashboards

Imagine that you are interested in a series of metrics that normally belong to different reports and that you want to check them periodically. How do you get them all in one place? Simple, just create a dashboard!

A dashboard is a flexible structure, a page in which to insert widgets that report the desired metrics. To create one, just go to Personalization> Dashboard> Create. You can choose to create a dashboard from scratch, starting from a blank sheet, or to use a pre-set dashboard (beginner dashboard).

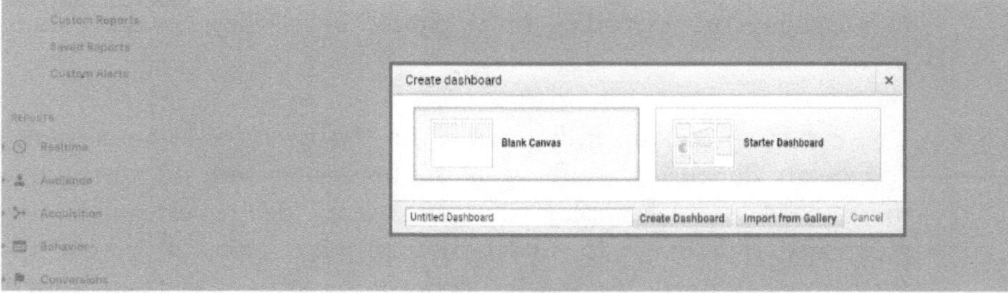

In the first case, the screen will immediately open to insert the first widget. As you can see, you can choose not only which metric to display, but also how (if as timeline, geographical map, pie chart, etc.); you can also view data in real-time. Once the first widget has been added, you can add more thanks to the "+ Add Widget" button just below the dashboard name, at the top left.

In the second case, you have a dashboard full of widgets that you can delete (X), customize (click on the pencil icon), or move (by dragging the desired widget).

At the top right there are two buttons: "Customize Dashboard" allows you to change the layout (the number of columns of the page and their proportions), "Delete dashboard" deletes it. Dashboards can also be shared: immediately under the dashboard name, next to the "+ Add Widget" button, you will also find the items "Share", "Email" and "Export". The first button allows you to share the dashboard in the form of a URL ("Share a link to model"), for all users of a view ("Share object") or in the Analytics Solutions Gallery. "Email" sends the PDF version of the dashboard via email, while "Export" downloads the PDF to your computer.

Audience reports

The Public section of Google Analytics contains a series of useful reports to provide an identikit of visitors to your website: age, gender, the countries in which they live, the language they speak, the devices and operating systems they use to connect, and even their interests.

The main reports are:

- Active Users Report
- Demographics and Interest Reports
- Geographic data reports

- **The Active Users report**

    The "Active Users" report shows users who have had at least one session on the site in the last day, in the last 7, 14 or 30 days. In other words, this report allows you to measure "site coverage" or "attractiveness". Are the marketing strategies that your site provides for returning users working? With the "Active Users" report you can find out!

- **Demographics and Interest Reports**

    The Demographics and Interests reports are probably among the most consulted among Google Analytics users.
    The former allows you to trace a demographic profile of users of the site since they provide information on age and gender; the latter indicates user preferences for certain types of content: the data is

grouped by "Affinity category", "In-market segment" and "Other categories"

How can this data help you?

- If you know all the information about your site's audience, you can understand if you are targeting the right target or not;
- You can implement more effective (and profitable) marketing and content marketing strategies, for example by targeting a specific segment, age group, or geographical area.

Important: Data from the Demographics and Interests reports is not available by default. For the property you are interested in, you must activate the option "Enable Demographics and Interests reports" in Administration> Properties> Property settings. Once the function is activated, you will have to give Analytics 24 or 48 hours to collect the data (provided that the site is large enough to allow it).

Geographical Data Report

Among the most useful reports of Google Analytics, there is certainly the Location report in Geographical data. By consulting it you will be able to find out from which continent, nation and even city users look at you. Tracking takes place (anonymously) through IP addresses. The report presents the classic table that allows you to cross the data of geographical origin with parameters such as "Sessions", "% new sessions", "New users", "Bounce rate", "Pages/session", "Average session duration" etc.

The Languages report, on the other hand, shows which language visitors of your site use (better to say: which language they have set as that of their browser). The Utility? If you have a multilingual site (because you offer your product/service in multiple countries) you can try to understand which markets work best, which ones are expanding or, vice versa, the geographical areas in which you are most in difficulty. All valuable information when it comes to setting up a business strategy!

Acquisition reports

Acquisition reports cannot be missing from a Google Analytics guide. It is, in fact, a very powerful and extremely important tool for verifying the effectiveness of multi-channel communication. What does it mean? It means that with the data contained in these reports you can understand what are the sources of traffic to your site and measure its performance, in terms of access or - we will see later - of objectives.

Means and sources

Before examining the main reports in detail, we need to clarify the concepts of Middle and Source, two fundamental indicators.

The means are the mechanisms that lead users to visit your site. They are distinguished in

- **Organic:** traffic that arrives on your site through free search on engines.
- **CPC:** acronym for Cost per Click, indicates the traffic generated by a paid campaign on search engines (AdWords).
- **Referrals:** traffic from a link to your site on another site (other than a search engine).
- **Email:** users who landed on the site through an email marketing campaign.
- **None:** this indicates the users who arrived at the site by directly typing its URL in the address bar.

A medium can have different sources. For example, if the medium is "organic", the source can be Google, Bing, Yandex etc.or if the medium is "referral", the source is the URL that led users to your site.

The Channel report

In Acquisition> All traffic> Channels we can measure the traffic coming from different channels. What is a channel? It is a sort of label with which Google goes beyond the concept of medium and groups of various sources of traffic. For example, the "social" channel can have sources such as Facebook, Twitter, and Linkedin.

To discover the sources of a channel, just click on it in the table that appears in the second half of the page. More details on the concept of a channel can be found at this link.

The Referral report

Always in Acquisition> All traffic, you can find the Referral report. It allows you to understand which other sites bring users to yours thanks to the presence of links.

You can deepen your analysis by clicking on the individual sources: in this way, you will precisely identify the URLs through which you receive traffic. Do you also want to detect landing pages? Simple: just add "Landing page" as a secondary dimension, and you're done: you will have more information to establish possible collaborations with the websites that link to you.

If you want to know how to get many external links to your website and also why this is fundamental to improve your online positioning, read my SEO guide!

Search Console reports

Google Analytics integrates perfectly with another fundamental web marketing tool offered (for free) by Google: Google Search Console. This is the first and most important SEO audit tool: Search Console allows you to detect errors that risk making your site not visible, to analyze the queries (i.e. search phrases) with which users find you on the web, landing pages and more.

Integrating Search Console with Analytics is therefore an indispensable move to have all the information relevant to your marketing strategy in one place.

How to connect Search Console with Analytics? Easy: go to Administration> Property Settings and, in the section dedicated to Search Console, find the corresponding property. (Don't have your Search Console account yet? Find out how to create and configure it here)

In this way, the Search Console report will show you landing pages, countries, devices, and search queries that users use to get to your site.

Behavior reports

Do you want to understand how users interact with your site? Take a look at the Behavior reports: you will find all the information about the page views, the average time spent on them, the bounce rate, and more. Perhaps the most interesting element of this category of reports concerns the flow of behavior: let's analyze it now!

- **The flow of behavior**

    Can you tell how users behave once your website has landed? Which pages are they browsing, which are they abandoning, and following which paths? All these questions are answered by a report called "Behavior Flow".

This report consists of a flowchart which highlights the nodes, connections, and exits that together form traffic flows.

- The nodes are the points of passage of the traffic and are marked in green. By clicking on them it is possible to highlight the traffic that passes through it and get a detail on the group (the pages grouped in this node).

- The connection is the path between one node and another and the volume of traffic generated.

- The exit is the point where the user leaves the flow.

Analyzing the flow of behavior provides interesting insights. The fact that for example, that users always leave the flow at the same point can indicate critical issues that, if resolved, improve the user experience and conversions.

Site Content reports

The relationship of users with the contents of your site is the subject of the Site content report. In the All pages are, for each page of your site, information useful to total page views, unique display (how many sessions that given page was viewed at least once), access (how many sessions began from that given page), the percentage of exits, and the bounce rate.

The pages are displayed by default based on the URI (the part of the URL that appears after the domain name), but it is possible to set the main size to "Page title" to display the title of each content as indicated in the source code.

The other reports

The behavior reports contain a lot of useful information to understand how your site is navigated. Since this Google Analytics guide is "basic", we will not examine them all in detail. Here is however a brief description

- **Content details** (in Site content) groups the pages by directory: it is a useful way (especially if the graph display is set to "pie") to check which sections of the site are most visited.

- **Landing pages** (under Site Content) displays the pages from which visitors entered your site (so-called "landing page").

- **Exit Pages indicates** the pages from which users have left the site. Pay attention to this report, especially if you have e-commerce: the fact that -

for example - many users leave the site from the purchase payment page could indicate some criticality, to be corrected to maximize results.

- **Events** are a report that allows you to monitor specific events (e.g. clicks on a video player or downloads). To monitor these elements, you have to carry out a series of options perfectly described in the official Analytics Guide:

GOOGLE FOR WEB MARKEITNG: CAMPAIGNS, GOALS, CONVERSIONS

What Google Analytics guide would this be if you didn't talk about how to monitor your campaigns, set goals, and measure the success of your AdWords ads? Analytics is in fact above all a marketing tool, and therefore these functions enhance its characteristics and usefulness.

Before diving into this new section, let's clarify the term "conversion". Conversion does not mean (only) "purchase": in the jargon of web marketing, this word indicates any action performed by the user that is relevant to your business. So if your site is t-shirt e-commerce, the conversion will coincide (also) with the purchase of a shirt; but if yours is a blog of - example - web marketing and your goal is to increase the mailing list, the conversion will also be every new subscription. (So, to go back to the e-commerce example: if you have a section dedicated to the newsletter and launch a campaign to get new subscribers to whom to offer exclusive promotions, conversions will also be the new subscriptions).

Well, now let's see how?

Monitor a web marketing campaign

Web marketing campaigns can be carried out with different tools. For example, advertising on social media, text ads on search engines, paid banners on other sites, emails. It doesn't matter which channel you choose; the important thing is that it is appropriate to the target and the result you want to achieve and, above all, that it is traceable.

Monitoring a web marketing campaign with Google Analytics is the best way to derive the data that allow you to understand if the strategy worked, where, why, on which audience, medium or source, etc.

Analytics monitors campaigns through the use of internal tags. What are these tags? They are pieces of information that are added to the URLs of the landing pages. When users click on these pages (for example because they are links promoted on Facebook or inserted in the text of a newsletter), the tracking code collects the data and sends it in special reports.

In this way, nothing of your campaigns will escape you!

Campaign Tags: the URL Creation Tool

Yes, but how are these tags made? And how can I insert them in the URL?

First, let's define them. There are 5 campaign tags and they refer to specific information:

- **Medium:** the technology used (mail, CPC, social, etc.);

- **Source:** the origin of the user depending on the medium (e.g. if the medium is a paid campaign on search engines, sources can be Google, Bing, Yahoo, etc.);

- **Campaign:** the name of the marketing campaign (eg "Promo summer 2017");

- **Content:** thanks to this tag, it is possible to differentiate the versions of the same promotion;

- **Term:** the keyword used for paid search campaigns;

You decide the values of these tags. How? Through the URL Creation Tool, available in the Google Help Center.

The Analytics Campaign URL Builder screen

This tool allows you to establish the tag-by-tag values and, above all, to obtain the URL duly modified and therefore ready to activate the Analytics reports. This is the URL that you will have to use in your campaigns!

But be careful: before proceeding with the campaign, test the link! A particular configuration of your site may block the functioning of these tags. Immediately after creating the custom URL, paste it in the address bar of your browser in incognito mode, and browse the site. If you have set goals (we'll see how later), take one of the relevant actions as well. After a few hours, in the Acquisition> Campaigns> All campaigns section, you can check that the campaign is active.

Goals in Google Analytics

So far we have seen how to track campaigns. How to track them accurately? How to measure the value they produce? Through the Goals!

For each goal, you will be able to view the total number of conversions and the conversion rate, i.e. the percentage of users who took that action. Not only that: you can also set up a "target funnel", or an ideal path that will help you understand where users abandon the conversion process.

- Create a goal

You can create a goal in Administration> View> Goals. You can only do this if you are an administrator of the view. You can create up to 20 goals.

By clicking on "New Goal", you can choose between a series of preset goals or a custom goal.

Analytics provides some predefined business goal templates, but you can also create a custom goal. Suppose we are monitoring contact requests for a form. We then select "Custom".
In the next screen, we are led to assign a name to the target (eg "Home request requests" if we want to monitor a form on the home page). "Objective area ID" is a numerical identifier to be associated with the objective, between 1 and 20. The objectives are grouped into 4 sets of objectives. Goal sets help to distinguish goals based on common characteristics (e.g. all filled out forms, all downloads, all purchases, etc.)

We then select the type of objective. We distinguish between:

- **Destination:** the achievement of a certain page of the site.
- **Duration:** a certain duration of a user's session.
- **Pages/screens per session**: a certain number of pages viewed by a user in a session.
- **Events:** specific action.

In our case, we select "Destination". Because? Because if our goal is to fill out a form, a quick way to measure it is to monitor how many people reach the thank you page that is activated after pressing the "Send Message" button. Attention, however: if there are different forms on the site, and I intend to track them all, each must have a separate thank you page, that is with a specific URL.

By clicking on "Continue" we access the "Objective details". In the "Destination" field, we select "equal to" and enter the URI of the thank you page (eg /thankyou1.html). If we want to set a value for each conversion, we activate the relative switch. For example, I can establish that each completed form is worth 1$; in the case of the sale of a product, in this field, I will enter the net profit that the sale provides me.

To monitor a specific channel, I activate the relative switch and insert the nodes of the path, each identified by a name and the URI of the page. If you set the first step as "mandatory", the "Funnel View" (Conversion> Goals> Funnel View) will track only those that start from that point.

Before saving the goal, I always recommend checking it: Google Analytics will show how often the goal could have been converted in the last 7 days.

Now that the goal has been created, you'll have to wait a few hours before Analytics shows you the reports. Goal metrics will be available in the Conversions> Goals> Overview reports. Objective data will also be available in other reports (e.g. Public or Acquisition).

Tracking of Google AdWords ads

AdWords is Google's platform for creating advertisements. These can be of two types: text or display. Text ads appear in Google search results when a user types a certain keyword (or query); display ads, on the other hand, consist of text, images, animation, or video and appear within a series of sites that make up the Big G Display Network.

Linking Analytics to your AdWords account is a smart choice because it allows you to analyze the involvement generated by your ads and tie it to other metrics (e.g. goals). How to do? Just go to Administration> Properties> AdWords Linking, and you're done.

- **Automatic coding**

Remember the URL builder tool we talked about above? Well, in the case of AdWords it is not necessary. This platform can automatically add campaign tags to the destination URL through the automatic tagging function.

This function allows you to add a series of information:

- **Query match type**: shows how a match is found between an AdWords keyword and a user's search query;

- **Ad group:** shows the ad group associated with the keyword / creative and the click;
- **Destination URL:** shows the AdWords destination URL configured in AdWords ads;
- **Ad format:** indicates whether the ad is text, display or video;
- **Ad distribution network:** shows the network used to publish the ad;
- **Placement domain:** is the domain on the Display Network where the ad was published;
- **AdWords Customer ID:** is the unique ID assigned to your AdWords account;

By analyzing this data in the Acquisition> AdWords reports, you can improve the performance of the campaigns by comparing, for example, the results of the different formats or by analyzing the various keywords.

In particular, keep an eye on the reports:

- **Campaigns**, useful for calculating the performance of active campaigns, which will be organized using the same names assigned in AdWords.
- **Keywords,** which shows the performance of keywords and keywords. Thanks to metrics such as bounce rate or conversion rate, you can significantly improve the performance of your campaign.

MODULE 21
TOOLS FOR DIGITAL MARKETING RESEARCH

Research is essential to the success of any digital marketing activity. Without proper planning and research, it is much harder to accomplish tasks, and sometimes even without success. Always research and plan and not only will it make your job easier but you will also learn a lot of new things along the way.

The most needed tools of Digital Marketers for 2020

GOOGLE TRENDS

Google Trends allows you to view the latest trends and data from Google and find out what the trends are in your area. Google Trends will give you an idea of what's going on in the world.
Simply go to the Google Trends website and type in the keyword or industry name you are interested in and search for. You can also add other data in parallel

so you can compare the results later. You can search by country, time period, category, and type of search, which includes a YouTube search.

GOOGLE KEYWORD PLANNER

So, there are more opinions about the Google Keyword Planner tool, there are people who love it and people who hate it and think the results are wrong. I'm not going to tell you what I think; I'm just going to tell you how you can use it in the best possible way.

What exactly is Google Keyword Planner? Google Keyword Planner is part of Google Adwords, which I will talk about later in this article. It is located in the "Tools" tab. You can choose one or more keywords, select the country and language you need, and see approximately how many times your target word has been searched.

You can see if the target word is ranked "High", "Medium" or "Low" and what is the amount of advertising for that word.

APP ANNIE

If you are an app creator or marketing manager for a particular business that has its own mobile app, you definitely need the Appannie tool. It is the best tool for tracking competitors in almost every store that has its own application.

The best feature in my opinion is "ASO" (App Search Optimization). It allows you to check exactly where your application is ranked on a particular keyword on the Google Play Store and Apple Store.

Based on the results of AppAnnie, you can edit the titles and descriptions of the application during the next update of the application. This way you can test and see which description works best.

SERPSTAT

Serpstat is also an amazing keyword search tool that I'm personally very happy with. The Serpstat tool is similar to the Ahrefs tool. I use this tool mainly for data comparison and because data for some countries are more accurate than other tools. Recently, Serpstat redesigned the interface and now the tool looks amazing.

You can also track competitors' keywords. The tool is super easy to use and you should check it out.

SIMILAR WEB

SimilarWeb is the first tool I use when I want to get a report on a particular website. This tool evaluates how much monthly traffic a page has, where it comes from, which countries, according to which keywords rank high, and a few more options. I usually use the extension in Google Chrome, because as I said, it immediately gives me information about a particular website, and I then decide whether I want to continue the research or not.

NIEL PATEL, QUIKSPROUT, KISSMETRICS

Neil Patel is the true definition of a super successful marketer. His articles are too long, but the content is great! He is an extremely successful entrepreneur and it is truly amazing that he unselfishly shares his knowledge and all the tricks he constantly uses to improve his business. This is a person you can definitely learn from and achieve too much.

MEDIUM

In my opinion, Medium is one of the best places to find interesting things to read and learn.
If you are on a website to learn but can't read or don't have time to read an article of 2-3-4 thousand words, there is a Google Chrome Extension that will do it for you:

The extension automatically adds a "Play" button at the bottom of your screen when you're on "Medium" and when you click the button, it starts reading the article. I use it a lot and I'm really happy.

BUZZSUMO

Buzzsumo is a tool for discovering new and current content. Its task is to analyze a certain topic that you will give it and it will show you the content that is best placed on the Internet. If you have a blog and want to discover certain topics that are currently relevant, just enter a certain phrase/keyword and it will take out everything related to you. The content that will show you is best ranked/liked/shared. You can even see who wrote the content on Twitter and you can contact them when you're ready.

Buzzsumo has launched the Question Analyzer tool to help you find the most popular questions asked through thousands of forums such as Amazon, Reddit, Quora, etc. All you have to do is enter a topic, keyword, or brand name and you can immediately see the most common questions posted online. The results are automatically filtered to show you the most frequently asked questions.

FACEBOOK AUDIENCE INSIGHT

One of the most powerful and valuable tools out there right now. As we know, Facebook has one of the best advertising systems because it has a huge amount of data for all of us. If you learn to use this tool, your job will become much easier and more profitable. The best part is that it's really easy to use and you won't waste days learning it. It can help you plan an ad for Facebook in the best possible way.

You can see how many people you can cover based on country of residence, interests, devices they use, behavior, habits, and even life events. It shows you demographic data and for some countries, you can even search by household income.

You can also see what other interests people have in your target group and which is the best way to cover them.

FACEBOOK ADS

As you know, Facebook is the largest social network in the world with an average of 25.5 billion visits per month. The average duration of a session is 16 minutes and 5 seconds. Because of this value of the company and the ability to collect data about your target group, Facebook is, in my opinion, the most powerful advertising network in 2020. If you don't use it for marketing purposes, you need to learn how to get started right away!

There are many types of ads that you can place on Facebook based on where your target group users are.

GOOGLE ADWORDS

Google Adwords is a tool that earned a record $ 67.39 billion in 2015, according to statista.com. It is one of the most widely used and complex advertising platforms to date. It recently got its redesign. Some people liked it, but some didn't. The truth is that not much has changed in terms of functionality. If you are a marketer you should definitely learn how to use it. At least the basics. It's no coincidence that some companies hire people who have mastered Google Adwords and pay them really well!

His abilities are enormous! You will need a lot of time to learn all the options that this tool has. I recommend browsing the program " Google Partners " Google Adwords is very important because you can use Google-linked channels through Google AdSense and achieve great results in Google Search. In this situation, you have the power to show users an ad for exactly what they are looking for at the moment. Conversion rates are much higher when the user sees an ad for something they are actually looking for.

GOOGLE ANALYTICS

There are many statistics on how many websites Google Analytics uses. In 2015, Marketing land found that Google Analytics was used by about 30-50 million websites.

Other sources, such as W3Techs, say that Google Analytics uses 54.9% of all websites. However many websites use it, it is one of the most popular and powerful analytics tools in the world and if you are a digital marketer, online entrepreneur, marketing manager, and even CEO, you must learn how to use it.

With Google Analytics you can track your users what is being done on your website. You can even find out which screen resolution they used?. You can create all kinds of reports and thus learn more about the people who use your services.

GOOGLE DATA STUDIO

Google Data Studio (beta) converts your data into information boards and reports that are easy to read, easy to share, and fully customizable.

One of the biggest challenges when working with data is to be able to manage and use all of our data. Google Data Studio greatly simplifies the process.

Once you have your raw data, it needs to be turned into useful and complete information so that it can be used. Google Data Studio converts your data into charts and information boards that make them easily readable and understandable for further management.

FB PIXEL HELPER

Just like with Google Tag Assistant, you can check if your Facebook Pixel is installed and set up correctly, and if the data it sends is OK.

GOOGLE TAG MANAGER

If you have a website and want to track and analyze multiple things at once, you must have many codes placed in different places on the website. They must be placed in sequence because you will surely want one function to be performed first and then another after it... It sounds really complex... No worries! Google Tag Manager takes care of all this.

Basically, you can put all your codes in GTM, and it will generate only one piece of code that you will put on your website. The whole process can be a bit complicated if you are not familiar with the basics of HTML and the background functionality of a website. But don't worry, there are a ton of free online tutorials to help you with this.

Check out this list on YouTube for Ryan Stewart's Google Tag Manager.

I hope it helps and you start using GTM. You will not need help in the future from developers to implement code snippets that previously seemed so complex. It will change your life, I promise.

DATA SCRAPER

With this tool, you can download any kind of data from a particular website. You just need to define your filters and download the data in the form of a document. I use it the most when creating campaigns in Google Adwords.

What I'm doing is telling Google to submit the first 100 results to me for a specific request, adding% var% at the end of the link, you download the results without any problem.
You can also use this Google Chrome extension.

FLATPACK

Flatpack is a drag-and-drop tool for designing web pages. Don't get me wrong, this tool can't be a replacement for a web designer or Front-end developer. With Flatpack, you can make a cultural web page in a relatively short time. It is quite easy to use.

This is a great tool for quick testing. The price is $ 18 and believes me it is nothing compared to the quality of the tool.I totally recommend it.

CANVA

If you are not a designer and you need pictures for your website, your ads, or social media then "Canva" is the ideal tool for you.

With Canva you can create a solid design for your needs in just a few minutes.

ADESPRESSO ADS

As far as I know, this started as a side project of AdEspresso and I think it's phenomenal.
With this tool, you can write a keyword or the name of a company and it will show you what type of ads they run.

DRIBBLE

My favorite website serves as a portfolio of designers. Here you can find scientific studies, animations, logos, and all kinds of designs. You can find huge companies that work with design, but also countless designers who work independently.

You can stay on top of modern trends and really learn a lot. Most of the things posted here are phenomenal!

BEHANCE

This is perhaps the most popular portfolio website for any type of design-related projects. If you want to be inspired by any theme, not just graphic design, but also architecture, typography, motion graphics, or anything related to design, this is definitely a place you must check.

Also on this site, you can find different designers that you can pay and work for you.

UNPLASH

This is a great website that has great and FREE images. You can find all kinds of pictures and ideas that you can use for your website, for sending emails, social networks, etc.

Another thing is that I really love the culture of the people behind this great project! Definitely, worth checking out this website, you won't be disappointed!

EVERNOTE

Evernote is a great place to store ideas. The best part is that you can sync it with all your devices. When you want to remember something and write it down on your phone, it immediately syncs with all your devices.

Another great thing is that you can share everything you have created with a friend and keep working together! This tool is not just for sewing notes. You can scan documents, attach PDF documents, and save important emails. All this will be saved on all devices where your Evernote account is active.

SLACK

You've probably already used Slack. This is a team chat platform that has been around for several years. There are two sides. People who think this tool destroys productivity and those who think it's very useful. There is much integration with the most popular tools used as a team. There are also bots with different functionalities.This tool can be very useful if you send a lot of emails.

"Here are 25 tools that are essential for all digital marketers and enthusiasts. Most of these tools are constantly used by me and trust me that if you learn how to use these tools, they will change your life.

"Through this book, you have learned many ways of digital marketing,
I always believe in learning, but learning is not enough, it is important to always practice what you teach, so I suggest to you that whatever you have learned from this book, keep trying it as much as possible"

Keep learning, keep practicing, and hope you have a bright future in the field of digital marketing.